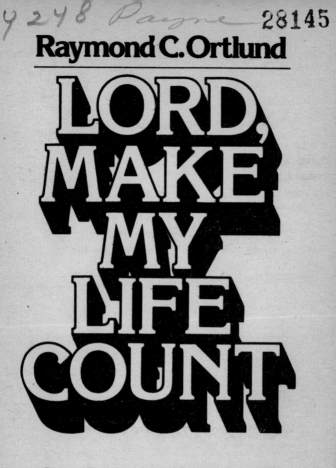

Raymond C. Ortlund

LORD, MAKE MY LIFE COUNT

Special Youth Edition of
Lord, Make My Life a Miracle

A Division
Glendale
EVANG
BRENTWOOD, CA

D0381479

To ANNE
. . . unbelievably wonderful wife,
whom God uses in making my life
a miracle.

Published by
Regal Books Division, G/L Publications
Glendale, California 91209

Library of Congress Catalog Card No. applied for
ISBN 0-8307-0348-9

The Scripture quotations are from:
  KJV—King James Version
  RSV—Revised Standard Version, copyrighted 1946 and 1952 by the Division of
  Christian Education of the NCCC, U.S.A., and used by permission.
  TLB—The Living Bible, Paraphrased (Wheaton: Tyndale House, Publishers, 1971).
  Used by permission.
  NASB—New American Standard Bible. © The Lockman Foundation, 1971. Used
  by permission.

CONTENTS

COMMITMENT THREE:

*Commit yourself to the world—your work
in it, your witness to it.*

A Teacher's Manual and Student Guide for
use with this book are available from your
church supplier.

The Birth of a Life-style: Three Priorities

It was the winter of 1968, and I was pastor of the Lake Avenue Congregational Church in Pasadena, California. We were going through all the proper motions of a Great Evangelical Church. Visitors would murmur all the right words about "great missionary emphasis" and "great youth program."

But my heart wasn't satisfied. There were too few "delivery-room" cries of newborns, too few victory songs at midnight.

I had exclaimed in anguish many times in my life, "I refuse to be an ordinary Christian!"

I had pounded the pulpit and said, "I refuse to be an ordinary pastor! I refuse to pastor an ordinary church!"

Then I read a sentence from Thomas Kelly that set my heart on fire. He prayed, "Lord, make my life a miracle."

Oh, God! That's it! You're the original Miracle, and I live in You. Why shouldn't my life be a miracle? Why shouldn't I be able to show others how to be miracles?

I talked of dissolving the church membership and asking everyone who meant business to join again. (Like at the Battle of the Alamo: "Who will step over this line?")

We met week after week, with lots of ideas. Lots of sawdust and a little gold!

But our God is a God of miracles. "Call on Me," He says, "and I will show thee great and mighty things, which thou knowest not."

At the early church service six Sundays later, I said to our people,

"I have a plan. We need to turn a new corner. We need a fresh start together as a people. Would you join me in three commitments? I'll be the first to sign my name:

"Number one: at whatever stage you are spiritually, commit your heart anew to the Person of God Himself in Jesus Christ.

"Number two: commit yourself to the Body of Christ, to be in a regular small group of believers, small enough so that you can be personally accountable to them for your growth, and personally responsible for their growth.

"Number two: commit yourself to the body of Christ, to be in a regular small group of believers, small enough so that you can be personally account-

2

able to them for your growth, and personally responsible for their growth.

Then I said, "If you're willing to commit yourself to these three priorities in this order, sign your name to it on the registration card."

Before the second service God gave me a name for the signers, borrowed from Elton Trueblood. We'd call them "The Company of the Committed." Bless 'em, the people in the first service didn't even know what they'd joined.

Nobody knew except my wife Anne that I'd been desperate enough to make a deal with God. "Lord, if five hundred people don't sign up for this, I'm leaving Lake Avenue Church."

Monday is our day off. I'm not supposed to be around the church at all, but—

Did I have a job, or didn't I?

I sneaked into the office of Virginia, my secretary. She grinned. "How about this stack of joiners of the 'Company of the Committed'?" The pile of cards looked gorgeous to me! There were six hundred!

What does God do through the little act of people putting their names on white cards?

It seems like nothing. But then, so does piling up a heap of stones, or killing a lamb for sacrifice. . . .

The forming of the Company of the Committed at Lake Avenue Church became a wide-running current of warmth and vitality through the river of the church membership. It was such a widening band that after a few years we quit talking about the Company of the Committed. Lake Avenue Church rent of warmth and vitality through the river of the church membership. It was such a widening band that after a few years we quit talking about the Company of the Committed. Lake Avenue Church had *become* a Company of the Committed. Sure, there have been ebbs and flows, and sure, we have lots of fringers, hangers-on and novices on their way to getting into the Company of the Committed. But our one-two-three commitment is the life-style of the Body, and the life-style of many hundreds of turned-on Christians within the Body.

It represents the most exciting concept I know. It can change your life as it has mine. It says, "My three life priorities are going to be—

1. God
2. Believers
3. My work in this world

In that order!"

In this book let me show you what I mean.

COMMITMENT 1

Wherever you are
spiritually, commit
your heart again
to God.

"Yes, yes," you say hastily. "I accepted Christ when I was twelve, and that's already settled. Now let's get on to the Body, to fellowship, to work, to priorities, to life-style, to all these fun things everybody's chatting about these days."

Wait! Stop! Be still! Be quiet!

You're nearsighted, my friend. Your eyes are focused on what's closest. So are the eyes of millions of other busy, nervous, frantic, activist Christians in this age.

Will you adjust your vision? Will you look beyond all that? Will you see the Lord, high and lifted up, seated on His throne, surrounded by worshiping ones? Will you dare to lift your eyes?

You'll be smitten. You'll realize you're profane.

You'll be separated from all your busy-busy, horizontally motivated brothers. You'll cry, "O God, my mouth is filthy, and I live among people with filthy mouths. I'm undone."

But oh, my friend! The sight of this Super Being will not crush you, but cleanse you. His fire will burn away all your filthiness, all your bitterness. (Yes, I'm talking to Christians.)

You'll feel so free, so clean, so exhilarated that when you hear God's challenge for service you'll be ready for . . .

Number two: attention to the Body, and
Number three: attention to your work in this world.
Don't rush past Number One.
This is the Blockbuster.
This, my Christian friend, may be your personal confrontation on the Damascus road.

1

LIVE WITH GOD

When Galileo discovered the truth of the earth's center, it caused all science to make some revisions. All that had been previously believed had to be adjusted to this new fact.

When you begin to see that the true center of life is in God, then all the rest of our lives must be adjusted to that new and true fact.

Someone said that the most fundamental thing anyone can do is to bring a man to God and leave him there. That's my desire! I want to get to God and stay there, and I want this also for you.

Thomas Kelly wrote,

"We are unhappy, uneasy, strained, oppressed, and fearful we shall be shallow.

"Over the margins of life comes a whisper, a faint call, a premonition of richer living which we know we are passing by. . . . We have hints that there is a way of life vastly richer and deeper than all this hurried existence, a life of unhurried serenity and peace and power.

"If only we could slip over into that Center! If only we could find the Silence which is the source of the sound!"[1]

One summer on vacation I stumbled onto the writings of Thomas Kelly, a recent Quaker. He was saying things my heart responded to, that I wasn't hearing from other twentieth-century evangelicals. I traced the people he quoted—George Fox and other early Quakers, as well as writers clear back to those of the thirteenth and fourteenth centuries.

I had always *believed* in the centrality of God; I had taught the *doctrine* of it. There are many movements that take this doctrine as their central theme and do a beautiful job with it—Torchbearers, Keswick and others. But to find those who talk about the *techniques* of living consciously "in God," you must go back to the old church fathers—someone like Brother Lawrence *(Practising the Presence of God)*—or you go to the Quakers.

You see, today we are activists. We love Christ, but we don't stay much around Him. We take gladly of God's forgiveness, but we don't have too much time to wait on God, or for God, or with God. We are on the move. We run into prayer, and then we say, "I've got to get on with life, on with real life."

How unaware we are of what "the real" really is!

In the fall we see flocks of geese heading south. They may land on a pond and feed for awhile; but soon, however pleasant that surrounding may be, there is an instinct that calls them out into the blue and down to the South—that calls them to their home.

Christian friend, do you feel in your heart a new tugging toward God? Do you feel that longing instinct, that you're not—in your day-by-day experience—all the way home yet? God is stirring you up; He is moving you. Up out of the pond! Keep pursuing!

After Thomas Kelly, I ran across the writings of Frank Laubach, in a little book called *Open Windows, Swinging Doors*. This "turned me on" some more about this, and I began to really see that in my own personal life there had been much lack. Frank Laubach was a missionary in the Philippines who, by the way, saw that millions were taught to read. This man wrote.

"For the past few days I have been experimenting in a more complete surrender than ever before. I am taking, by deliberate act of the will, enough time from each hour to give God much thought. Yesterday and today I have made a new adventure, which is not easy to express. I am feeling God in each movement, by an act of will. . . .

"You will object to this intense introspection. Do not try it, unless you feel dissatisfied with your own relationship with God, but at least allow me to realize all the leadership of God I can. I am disgusted with the pettiness and futility of my unled self. If the way out is not more perfect slavery to God, then what is the way out? Paul speaks of our liberty in Christ.

"I am trying to be utterly free from everybody, free from my own self, but completely enslaved to the will of God every moment of this day."[2]

I've been living this recently with much failure, and now and then a little bit of success. I use an alarm wristwatch that I was given by dear Wycliffe missionaries in Vietnam after ministering there. I put it either on the hour or the half hour just to remind myself, "It's time, boy, to reach up to heaven. Get up there! Draw near and enjoy the presence of God. Don't get bogged down with everything here." This is what my alarm is for, and when it doesn't bother others, I set it.

But I find I don't need it so much now, because the Holy Spirit has been wonderful in helping me to be aware of God.

You know, there were a couple of sins in my life that I couldn't break. I really couldn't! They were mastering me. But when I find myself in the presence of God, those sins don't belong. It's amazing what the presence of God does. He makes those things incompatible with Himself; they're not important anymore, and they've lost their hold on me.

Praise God!

Sin will keep you from God's presence, or God's presence will keep you from sin.

Jesus began His earthly life based on the promise "God with us," Matthew 1. He ended His earthly life with the promise, "Lo, I am with you," Matthew 28. At both ends, the promise of the Presence.

And not just the Presence *with*, but the Presence *within*. As the infant Saviour was placed into Mary and formed in her womb, so Paul cries out in Colossians, "Oh, I travail so that Christ may be formed in you!" You commit your body to Him that you might become His temple, the housing of God Himself—"Christ in you, the hope of glory."

There is so much that's rich here. I feel as though I'm barely touching on it. But God calls us to live *with Him.* This is not the idea of the omnipresence of God. It isn't the idea that I invited Jesus to come into my heart. That's wonderful, and the omnipresence of God is wonderful, but that's not what I'm talking about.

I'm talking about consciously, continually, living in the presence of God. Going in and out and finding pasture, as it were. Speaking with Him, talking with Him, enjoying Him, loving Him—rejoicing, praising, crying, complaining—all those things, in the presence of God.

Strong's *Theology* makes this comment:

"The majority of Christians much more frequently think of Christ as a Saviour *outside of them* than as a Saviour who dwells within."

We think of Christ as in heaven, 'way up there.

Now, here is our desk with a pile of papers we are trying to go through, while the phone is ringing off the hook.

Or, there are house chores to be done, somebody just spilled orange juice on the floor, and we've got to be at a youth meeting in five minutes.

Or we're in a classroom, and there's a paper due tomorrow morning or it's one point off your grade.

There are so many immediate *now* problems, and they get first "dibs" on our attention because *we think they're closest!* We haven't yet learned that "in Him we live and move and have our being." We don't understand that He is closer than hands or feet. We haven't yet learned to *live from the inside out.*

My friend, *Christ is in you* far more really, far more present, than all that which is going on around you!

12

He is closer than any problem! If you are living moment by moment with this great awareness of God within, everything else will be truly revolutionized.

Within! Within!

Most Christians would say, "Of course I know He's there." But educators say we haven't really learned something until there's changed behavior.

When Jacob ran from Esau he slept that night and had a great dream. When he woke up he exclaimed, "Why, the Lord is in this place, and I didn't even know it!"

Is that really true—experientially true—with you? Jacob was so engrossed with his problems with his brother, and he was pell-mell on the run. Through a dream God brought him up short—to see Himself.

Maybe for you—through these words?

It could be that you're feeling frustrated, that this sounds fine but it's just an unattainable goal, because there are so many demands upon your life. Maybe someday when you retire; but right now, you feel so pulled, so splintered.

Thomas Kelly says,

"We are trying to be several selves all at once, without all of our selves being organized by a single, mastering life within us.

"Each of us tends to be, not a single self, but a whole committee of selves. There is the civic self, the parental self, the financial self, the religious self, the society self, the professional self, the literary self. . . ."[3]

But God calls us first of all to Himself. There we find integration; we find unity; we find simplicity. One Lord, one faith, one work! There is a singularity about Him, and there must also be a singularity about the life that is lived *in Him*.

Kelly goes on,

"I think it is clear that I am talking about a revolutionary way of living. Practicing the Presence isn't something to be added to our many other duties, and thus make our lives yet more complex.

"The life with God is the center of life, and all else is remodeled and integrated by it. . . ." Everything is at hand, right here at the center. All power, all peace, all wisdom for moment-by-moment choices. We're moving into the practical, nitty-gritty how-to of the established fact of the indwelling of the Holy Spirit. When you catch it, you'll live from the center out, rather than from the outside in.

When you live from the outside in, what happens to you inside? You get all tense and tied up. You're like a boxer waiting for the next punch. You're living, reacting to one situation, then reacting to the next one, and so on—happy or unhappy depending on each external circumstance.

What a shame! That's no different from the way an atheist lives!

George Fox wrote,

"It is a wonderful discovery to find that you are a temple, that you have a church inside of you, where God is. In hushed silence, attend to Him. 'The Lord is in His holy temple!' "

King David said to young Mephibosheth, "You and Ziba divide the land between you."

And Mephibosheth answered, "Look, let Ziba take all the land. Let me just live with you, David, and eat at your table. That's all I want!"

Oh, that's the way to be! Longing for God Himself! Nothing but God. That's why God could use Moses. Moses cried, "I don't want angels, I don't want substitutes, I just want God!"

If you don't know the "hereness" of God—then, my friend, you haven't begun to find out His relevance for your Christian life.

Psalm 73:28, "But for me, it is good to be near God; I have made the Lord God my refuge, that I may tell of all Thy works."

Psalm 16:11, "In thy presence is fulness of joy. At thy right hand there are pleasures forever more."

God said to Moses, "My presence shall go with you, and I will give you rest."

Oh, the joy, the comfort of living with God! Dear friend, don't miss it!

This isn't a single commitment; it's a moment-by-moment commitment. It calls you from "scattered-mindedness" to single-mindedness.

How long is the great mass of God's people going to be so preoccupied with the fringes, the externals, the side issues?

God is so patient. Think how many times He has flashed lightning across the sky. Through the ages it would splinter huge trees. It would run a cow down a path, while men watched and wondered.

All the time God was trying to tell men something.

One stormy day a man finally went out with a kite and a key. All heaven was probably bending over saying, "All these years we've been trying to tell them about electricity. Look, look, he's got it! At last, he's got it!" And soon the world lit up.

How long, how long you and I have been vaguely

15

aware—theoretically aware—of God's presence with us! I think all heaven's waiting, and perhaps saying, "I think they might get it. Look, look, maybe at last they're going to get it!"

Christian young person, you may have been saved for three, five, fifteen years. Maybe at last you're going to get it!

The Christian life is to be lived from the center out, with God. How could you have missed it? Live from the center out. At the center is Jesus Christ and all His glory in you.

Begin the sweet discipline of acknowledging Him, moment by moment. Live with Him, have a running conversation going with Him, rejoice in Him.

Have you got it?

Then . . .

1. Begin to watch for God's presence with you. Keep a 3x5-inch card in your pocket or purse and jot down situations where you're aware of His presence.

2. Help remember God within you by saying each time you hear a bell or horn, "Thank you, God, for being within me."

3. Find a Christian friend and share the excitement of having God with and within you both. Call each other several times in the next week to encourage each other with reminders of this exciting fact!

4. Stop right now and talk to God about it. Tell Him how you feel about His being with and within you. Ask Him to help you relax in the awareness of this life-changing truth.

2

BE GOD-CENTERED

T. J. Bach was the leader of The Evangelical Alliance Mission—one of the great Christians of this century. He so lived in the presence of God that he would just be in and out of God's presence as he was in and out of the presence of other people.

Some of the men of our church were recounting stories of him the other morning. If you said to Dr. Bach, "I think I'm going to town this afternoon," he would say, "Lord, bless my friend as he goes to town. What time are you going?"

None of this bow-your-head-close-your-eyes-fold-your-hands sort of thing. He was just talking, and God was in it all.

You say, "But isn't that really kind of eccentric?"

Well, let's think about what it means to be eccentric.

Your life is like a wheel. The rim constantly moves about in the affairs of life—school, work, home, and so on. The hub is the center: that's the deeper "you," where you're believing, feeling, forming opinions, deciding issues.

A devotional book of the fourteenth century, *The Cloud of the Unknowing,* says:

"On one level we may be . . . meeting all the demands of the external affairs. But deep within, behind the scenes, at a profounder level, one may also be in prayer and adoration, song and worship, and a gentle receptiveness to divine breathings."

At the hub of your life, Christian young person, you have a choice: you can be God-centered—Christocentric—or you can be eccentric. The eccentric man is the man who is a bit off-center. How does he get that way? He will be eccentric if anything but God is central.

Anything but God.

Now, you want a Christian life that's meaningful. Of course you do. What is it that will help you have a meaningful life? You say, "Well, I'll go to a good, sound church. Surely this is the way to purpose and satisfaction."

You find a church, and it's exciting. Things are happening. A bright, happy spirit is there; God is at work. You say, "This is it!"

You throw yourself into youth activities and Sunday School classes—but after a year or two you say, "Well, a lot of these people are no better than I am, and some of them have worse problems than I have."

At this point you get restless again. It doesn't mean

you leave the church, but you begin to look for something else, something deeper. . . .

You hear of a special study held by some people who meet in a home and listen to somebody's tapes, and you think, "Why haven't I heard of this before? How come no one has told me about this?" And you say, "Soul, rejoice! Your search is over. This is it!"

So your life focuses on this new activity, this specialization. And it's wonderful; it's biblical. But soon you find that it doesn't really take care of everything, and you're still restless in your soul. You feel dry and empty.

Then one day a friend who seems to be full of joy says to you, "What you really need is a certain Christian experience." You think, "That must be true. That's exactly what I need." So you go to the place where these people are having this experience, and they all seem happy and rejoicing—such a great place. And you say, "Hallelujah! This is *it!*"

And you try to get "it" too, and all the group urges you on. They're rooting for you—and they say, "You've got to have more faith. Let go! Give up! Relax!"

Finally you get "it." You have this great experience and you say, "This has to be it. This must be it!"

Eventually the old restlessness creeps back.

Why?

Because all the time you were looking for *it,* and not for *Him!*

You see, the church itself must never be "front and center" in your life. Nor an experience—you mustn't be experience-centered. A specialization or a true, good doctrine must never be central. *God Himself* must be central. Anything else will make you eccentric—off center.

Here's a factory. All over it are wheels—huge wheels, little wheels, medium wheels—and they are all turning. The factory is running. Everything runs smoothly in the factory, because all the wheels are on center.

Here's another factory, with good wheels, well-made wheels, important wheels—but each wheel is just a bit off center. And when that factory begins to operate at 7:30 on a Monday morning, look out! There'll be all kinds of clattering and squeaking, and all kinds of smells of burning bearings. The place is shaking to pieces!

You know, this factory is like many a church. Everyone is doing his "thing."

There's a wheel over here squeaking away saying, "You've got to witness. Everybody's got to witness."

And there's another wheel smoking away, saying, "You've got to get liberty from the law!" Around it goes: "Liberty from the law, liberty from the law, liberty from the law. . . ."

Another wheel over here is groaning, "Second coming, second coming, second coming," and another, "Missions, missions, missions. . . ."

Now, all of their emphases are right and good, but if they're central, those Christians are eccentric! No wonder the average church is full of bumping and jostling.

How can you tell if you're eccentric? Well, examine yourself. If you follow any leader, any movement, any church, any doctrine, and make this central to your life and thinking, my friend, you're eccentric. You're spiritually off balance.

Second Corinthians 5:14 and 15 are so important. They say that Christ ". . . died for all, that those who live might live no longer for themselves, *but for Him,* who for their sake died and was raised." (*RSV*)

God alone is the balanced Person. God the Father, God the Son, God the Holy Spirit—they alone are really whole. God alone is sufficient in Himself. We have been so constructed as His people that we are only whole, we are only sufficient when all our lives are revolving around Him. We must be God-centered.

Many Christians find life so lopsided. Their lives are that wheel, but with too much attention given to the circumference. They are dependent on those who are outside of them, instead of dependent on God who is that "Holy Within." He must be the hub, the focus, the purpose.

This calls for a "centralized government" in our life. In Matthew 6:33 Jesus is talking about all the circumference things of life—food, clothing, and so on—and He says, "Seek ye first the Kingdom of God (the government of Christ) and all these things will take care of themselves. They will be added to you."

David wrote, "As the hart panteth for the water brook, so pants my soul for Thee, O God!" (Ps. 42:1).

"That in everything," wrote Paul, "He might be pre-eminent" (Col. 1:18). Then everything else takes its proper perspective.

Does something tug at you that says, "Oh, but surely I can have the best of two worlds—all of the circumference and God at the hub, too."

When Francis of Assisi was a young man, it was

said of him that when other young men ran away to the world, he ran away to God. No wonder everyone is quoting him, singing his songs.

Hebrews 11:6 tells us:

"He that cometh to God must believe that he is, and that *he is the rewarder of them that diligently seek him.*" (*KJV*)

My Christian friend, if you have not diligently sought after God in your life, really gone hard after God, to make Him central, to give Him preeminence—it may be because deep down, deep down in your heart, *you do not believe* that He is the rewarder of them that seek Him.

The big lie from the world and from the pit of hell itself is that God is not a good rewarder; that if you really follow hard after Him, you'll miss some of the "kicks" of life. Some of the "goodies."

You've been sold a bill of goods.

Only in God, *only in God* is there reward. Hear it—only in God.

Isaiah 26:3 says this to us, "Thou wilt keep him in perfect peace, whose mind is stayed on Thee." That's "practicing the Presence," my friend. That's holding God in central place in your heart.

And here's another snare: even as we think about being God-centered, our tendency is to want it "for me"—so I can have this "perfect peace"—and "I" am still in the center! I want the experience because it will make me a top-quality, grade-A Christian on the top of the pile—and at that point God is not attended to and waited upon and sought for what He is.

Oh, our motives, our motives.

But let me tell you something: you were made for this. You can go on lopsided through life if you want to, banging and squeaking on your way; that's your choice. But you were made to have Christ at the center.

Augustine said, "Our hearts are restless, O God, until they rest in Thee."

Christian, you can choose to invite God into the very center of your life, and let life flow outward from that inner core. You can "center down," as the Quakers say, on God Himself, if you want to—so that Christ becomes absolutely everything to you.

That's what F. W. M. Meyer did, that he could write,

    "Christ's! I am Christ's!
    And let that Name suffice you.
    Aye; and for me
    He greatly hath sufficed."

This is how it affected one humble London tailor, John Woolman:

"When too many customers came, he sent them elsewhere, to more needy merchants and tailors. His outward life became simplified on the basis of an inner integration.

"He found that we can be heavenly men and women, and he surrendered himself completely, unreservedly to that blessed leading, keeping warm and close to the Center."

George Fox, the founder of Quakerism about 1600, had this kind of itch for God: not to know religion, but God in Christ Himself. He went everywhere seeking from ministers, priests and laymen—anyone who could possibly tell him how he might know God.

His relatives said, "What you need, George, is to get married."

A priest advised him to smoke tobacco and to sing Psalms.

Another minister got angry and wouldn't even answer him because he stepped in his flower bed.

Another told him that what he really needed was some medicine and a good blood-letting!

Obviously, seminary training didn't hold the answer. Eventually Fox came to write:

"Unless you know God, immediately, every day communing with Him, rejoicing in Him, exulting in Him, opening your life in joyful obedience toward Him, and feeling Him speaking to you and guiding you into ever fuller obedience to Him—you aren't fit to be a minister." (Or, I might say, even to be a Christian.)[4]

Now, this takes faith. "That Christ may dwell in your hearts by faith," says Paul in Ephesians 3:17. He means that the indwelling Christ and the enjoyment of Him continually, requires an attitude of believing, an attitude of faith; that you really stay close to where the action is.

It's in God, my friend! It isn't anywhere else. That's "where it is"—in God.

You don't have to keep tabs on the Christian fire lest it go out—defending, fanning it. My friend, the fire is God. You only need to keep close to the fire. So do I.

Only those who know God, who get with God, who go with God in their daily life experiences, ever get to know the elegance of life—the elegance of life in God.

Brother Lawrence was a lame young man. He went into a monastery so that he might somehow atone for the fact that he was such a clumsy person.

But he was hungry for God. In the monastery he was put to work washing the floors and pots and pans of the kitchen. And it was he who in the midst of this "practiced the presence of God."

Brother Lawrence said,

"For me the time of action does not differ from the time of prayer, and in the noise and clatter of my kitchen, while several persons are calling for as many different things, I possess God in as great tranquility as when upon my knees."

When he was dying, his friends asked him what he was thinking about and he replied,

"I am doing what I shall do through all eternity— blessing God, praising God, adoring God, giving Him the love of my whole heart. It is our one business, my brethren, to worship Him and love Him, without thought of anything else."

If you are seeking a richer life, as I'm sure you are, you want something grander for the future than you've known in the past. God bless you! That's the hunger for God put in your heart by Him.

Listen, be like the disciples! You have toiled all night and taken nothing. Now let down your nets. Go after Him. Go into the deeps. (See Luke 5:1-11.)

And how do you do it? Well, just begin right where you are.

Inwardly begin to adore God. Begin to praise Him at the very depths of your being. Right now just say, "Lord, I love You. I praise You. I adore You! I want to live in Your presence."

Tomorrow morning when you get up, say, "Lord, here we are. What are we going to do today? I want to be with You all day long."

"Fairer than morning,
  Lovelier than daylight;
 Dawns the sweet consciousness—
  I am with Thee!"

Then all day long, behind the scenes, at the very deepest level, hold conversation with God.

As you walk down the street or sit in a classroom, ask God's blessing on those you see.

As you stop at a stop light or start your homework, express your love to Jesus.

As you go into your own home, "Dear God, today will You bless this home—and me, as I go in."

And as you go from here to there, "Praise to God. Thy will be done."

Keep the conversation running. It will take no extra time, my friend. It will take *all* your time.

And when you fail?—when you get clever again, when you assert your own way—well, don't spend lots of time groveling over it. Get up and go on. Go to God, and get on with Him again.

We are so success-centered. It's hard to have the patience to develop this quality in life. You know, on our television programs every mystery is solved in just twenty-eight minutes. And all the ladies' laundry problems are solved in sixty seconds!

But living with God takes time. You probably don't have gray hairs and have not lived long with the Lord; you know it takes time to grow deep with God. Oh, you'll need to keep at it. Keep there, keep in close, dear friend. Know what it is to grow graciously in the presence of the Lord. You'll succeed! Oh, I've failed so often. But the little bit of success I know is too good to give up.

This is not a self-improvement scheme. It isn't for you; this is for God! This is to gather ourselves around Him, and give Him glory and pleasure. This is the *God*-centered life.

What if you sin? You go to His presence anyway. Brother Lawrence said, "Lord, I'll keep doing the same thing all the time, unless You help me."

And then relax. "It is God that worketh in you," says Philippians 2:13, "both to will and to do of His good pleasure."

Think a minute about T. J. Bach. He was the only one who was *on* center! The world around him thought he was eccentric. My friend, *they* were the eccentric ones!

Do you fear becoming a fanatic? It's true that you won't be following a huge crowd if you live this way. But Kelly said:

"Better to run the possible risk of fanaticism by complete dedication to God, than to run the certain risk of mediocrity by 20 percent dedication. Better to run the risk of being examined by a psychiatrist than to measure our lives by our mediocre fellows. The prophets come to the world and say, 'Thus saith the Lord.' They don't say, 'Thus saith the majority'!"[5] My Christian friend, I call you to God.

Begin putting God at the center of your life right now:

1. In large letters on a 3x5-inch card write, "Go with God today, all day long. Ask *Him* to be the center!" Post the card on your mirror or some other

place where you will see it first thing every morning.

2. This week, whenever you see a wheel, stop to think about who is the center of your life, and to remember again Christ's desire to have you base life upon Him and His love.

3. List three times each today and three times tomorrow when you will spend time loving God—when you will acknowledge God's presence, praise Him for being God, and ask Him to be the center of your life. These may be while walking to school, going to class, or at a meal—any time you can think and pray.

Today	Tomorrow
(1)	(1)
(2)	(2)
(3)	(3)

4. Remember the Christian friend you called and shared with after reading chapter 1? Share with that friend what you have now learned about living a God-centered life. Ask that friend to encourage you and call to see how you are doing at making God center.

5. Stop right now and talk to God about your desire to have Him at the center of your life. Tell Him your desires; share with Him your fears of failure; allow Him to remind you of His love and His desire to bless you.

3
WORSHIP IN PRIVATE

There's one prime, basic, all-important place in your life where the rubber really meets the road.

At this place, my friend, you win or lose—you make it or your don't.

The place I'm talking about is where you go down on your knees, where you shut out all the rest of the world, and you and God, just the two of you, get together.

It has to be honest between you and Him.

It has to be regular, at least once a day.

And it has to be fought for, clawed and scratched for—or it will never happen.

As sweet as life is to live with God moment by moment—and that's where it all begins—that doesn't rule out your need for a consistent encounter where it's just God and you.

George Mueller, the man of great faith in nine-teenth-century England, shared his reason for spiritual power:

"The first thing to be concerned about was not how much I might serve the Lord, but how I might get my soul into a happy state, and how my inner man might be nourished. . . .

"I began therefore to meditate on the New Testament from the beginning, early in the morning. The first thing I did, after having asked in a few words the Lord's blessing upon His precious Word, was to begin to meditate on the Word of God, searching out of it, not for the sake of public ministry of the Word, not for the sake of preaching on what I had meditated upon, but for obtaining for my own soul."[6] You don't get food for your soul by osmosis! You can hear others talk of it; but until you regularly take in that delicious Word of God, you're under-nourished!

It was important for Christ. That in itself should make us go after quiet times with God. Think of it. Jesus took large hunks of time to be alone with His Father.

"Early in the morning, while it was still dark, He arose and went out and departed to a lonely place, and was praying there alone" (Mark 1:35). Evidently even the eternal Christ needed quiet periods of prayer. "He Himself would often slip away to the wilderness and pray" (Luke 5:16).

How nice of the Holy Spirit: He encourages us to spend time alone with God by showing us that Jesus did it!

It's not easy for us to comprehend, of course. Jesus

was the Son of God; why was it necessary? He was "with God; He was God." He "practiced the presence of God" in that utter and complete way that Psalm 16:8–11 prophesied:

"I have set the Lord always before me (says the Son, talking about the Father). Because he is at my right hand, I shall not be moved. Therefore my heart is glad, and my glory rejoiceth: my flesh also shall rest in hope. For thou wilt not leave my soul in hell; neither wilt thou suffer thine holy one to see corruption. Thou wilt show me the path of life: in thy presence is fulness of joy; at thy right hand there are pleasures for evermore!" (*KJV*) Even though He "lived and moved and had His being in God" in a unique way, Jesus still had to get away for quiet. He had to shut out the world for large hunks of time and communicate with the Father with no interruptions.

You say, "But He didn't live in the twentieth century!" My friend, we all have time for what we really want.

Choose a quiet place and a particular time for this daily event. You may not be able to keep the schedule every day; but work at it. Anytime becomes no time. Fix a daily appointment with God. Write it into your date book!

If I sound like the professional who's had all this mastered for years, let me tell you, Ray Ortlund sweats it out. There are plenty of pressures on a pastor's time. Through the years I've wavered back and forth between frustration and some success.

A few months ago I got good and desperate (I think God loves that!) and said, "Okay, Lord, it's going to be 5:15 every morning. That sounds like a time when there should be a minimum of visitors and phone interruptions."

Ugh! Do you know what the world looks like at 5:15 A.M.?

Do you know how hideous an alarm can sound then?

Do you know how luscious the bed feels at that hour? Before long I knew that the secret of getting up early was going to bed early! That's not easy in these crazy days. But here's where I had to plan my week with care. If meeting God was top priority, then other events would have to fit in, after and around. Period!

I began with "gusto." It was good. It was so rewarding that even the problem of afternoon fatigue (and making time for a nap) were worth the success I enjoyed. Now, six months later, it's not all success—but it's right, and I like it.

Frankly, as I look back over this period I don't see myself sprouting wings—but, praise God, I do sense He is quietly winning victories in my life. That makes it worth it all.

Whenever God and you are to meet together is up to you and Him. Let me warn you though: when you can't, or you fail to keep the appointment, don't beat yourself for it. After all, who are you to think you can be so perfect or consistent? And who am I? But by His strength, keep at it!

The goal of your Bible reading can be reached by asking the same two questions that Paul asked on the Damascus Road:

"Who art Thou, Lord?"

32

"What wilt Thou have me to do?" (See Acts 22:8-10, *KJV*.) In that holy time before the Book, have a double goal—to know God, and to obey Him.

What is the process of getting to this goal? Pray for understanding, and then read through your chosen passage for the day. Ask yourself what you learn in that passage about God or Christ. Don't hurry. Don't quit too soon. "Who art Thou, Lord?"

Also observe what you see is God's will for you. "What wilt Thou have me to do?" Then pray it into your day's plans.

Then have a structured, diligent prayer time. When I pray I like to use the simple acrostic of the word "Acts":

A—Adoration
C—Confession
T—Thanksgiving
S—Supplication (for others and yourself)

You learn to pray by praying. Use your head and your heart. When you pray, think! It helps greatly to talk out loud, so you voice with meaning your heart's desires. Really work at avoiding clichés! God must get tired of our dull sameness.

I like to plot my day in prayer. The two of us run through my appointments together and cover them all, even to the unknown interruptions. When I thank Him for interruptions before they ever happen, I find I handle them better. (They're part of your "Plan A," Father!)

As I was writing this, a pastor friend dropped in. Quiet time in the study is at a premium, but I found our conversation a real delight. What's more, as I committed it all to God while it was happening, he got to the point of his visit right away and I was back to work again. How important it is to hang in there with God and then feel Him enable me to hang loose. It surely beats any other way I know.

A medical doctor friend was on a retreat with our college gang recently. They were studying private prayer and practicing it. As he watched them go hard after God he said to the minister to students, "If my patients did this, half of them would never need come to me."

My wife Anne and I often feel the need to seek the Lord for a longer period, for a day or part of a day, the two of us alone together with God. We bring a hymnal and our Bibles, and we have a time. Sometimes the mountains call us, sometimes the beach, but we alternate times. We have a day of refreshing in the Word, singing, talking and praying together and separately.

It's so good to check up on our marriage. "How am I doing as a husband?" She can "shoot straight" in the cushioned atmosphere of prayer. And I can take it without getting up-tight. "How do you sense I'm doing in my life with the Lord? How can I improve?"

Try a day of prayer! It's refreshing and lifting. Make your own outline of what you should cover. Choose a Bible passage and work on it; make a list of subjects you need to pray through.

If Jesus did it . . .

"Now ye are clean through the Word. . . ." John 15:3. (*KJV*)

"The entrance of Thy Word giveth light" (Ps. 119:130, *KJV*).

Oh, the flavoring, the seasoning that God gives a life shot through with times with Him!

"When the Council saw the boldness of Peter and John, and could see that they were obviously uneducated non-professionals, they were amazed and realized what being with Jesus had done for them" (Acts 4:13, *TLB*).

"Lord, I have shut the door;
  Speak now the Word
Which in the din and throng
  Could not be heard;
Hushed now my inner heart;
  Whisper Thy will,
While I have come apart,
  While all is still."

It's really up to you. It's where the rubber meets the road.

Want to start working on it right now? Then:

1. Stop and plot the rest of today in prayer. Cover everything from work, duties and classes to conversations, meals and going to bed.

2. Write out a schedule for the next seven days and plan when you will spend time alone with God in prayer and study.

3. Begin to meditate on God's Word. Read it, think about it, take notes on it, memorize parts of it. Ask, "Who are You, Lord?" and "What would You have me do?" Begin with Psalm 145 and John 15:1-11, studying only as much of each passage as you can do well in that day.

4. If you want to do a longer study and don't know where to begin, try these books: John, Colossians, then Romans.

4
WORSHIP
IN PUBLIC

It's like the weather: everybody talks about it, but nobody really does much about it—this matter of worshiping. Thousands go through the motions every Sunday. A few are worshiping; most are just "playing church."

You've got to think about public worship. The task before you, Christian, is to *worship*—every week! Not to go to church every week and have the experience of true worship once a year, or almost never. But every time you go, to have learned the cleansing, satisfying art of public worship.

When Jesus came to earth He announced,

"The hour is coming, and now is, when the true worshipers shall worship the Father in spirit and truth; for such people the Father seeks to be His worshipers. God is a spirit; and those who worship Him must worship in spirit and truth" (John 4:23, 24, *NASB*)

Worship is the highest and noblest act that any person can do. When men worship, God is satisfied! "The Father seeketh such to worship Him." Amazing, isn't it? And when you worship, you are fulfilled! Think about this: why did Jesus Christ come? He came to make worshipers out of rebels. We who were once self-centered have to be completely changed so that we can shift our attention outside of ourselves and become able to worship Him.

"It ain't easy!"

Worship is top priority. Everything, absolutely everything, must be put aside to do this thing that God has called you to do. Worship is lofty business—but, friend, we do it so poorly.

I'm amazed at several obvious ways that our poverty in worship is displayed. Many Christians don't even show up with regularity. A person may say, "Well, I just don't get anything out of it."

You get nothing out of it?!

You get nothing out of the Word of the eternal God?!

You get nothing out of the great hymns of the church?!

You get nothing out of prayer through Jesus Christ to God Almighty?!

Then it's because you don't know how to put anything into it. It shows our deep misunderstanding of what worship is all about.

Or a person may say, "I'm tired. It's the only day I get off during the week." Friend, that's the only day you've got *on!* You'd better be "on," because worship is the meaning of the whole thing of living. If your job makes you too tired to worship God, quit your job. Find another.

And here's a subtle thing: our wonderful emphasis on fellowship has contributed to our deep poverty in worship! Think of that! We must cherish fellowship—it's good. But we must continually magnify worship—it's the best, much higher than anything else we can do. Too often we come to meet each other and miss meeting God. We chat with each other, but never really speak to God.

I believe that the problem is that we've never really learned the importance of worship. It's never really "come home" to us.

Can you imagine, some even go to Sunday School or even teach in Sunday School, but they don't go to a worship service! This completely amazes me. What if a child spent his entire childhood in his classroom at school with no home, no mother, no deep level of communication, no loving arms?

Something else that shows our poverty in worship is the attitude in which we come. You think it doesn't show? It does! Some come and fold their arms and lean back, look around, and kind of evaluate the situation. "How is the preacher doing today? His trousers are pressed pretty good. How do things look up in the choir?"

Friend, let me tell you something: you may have been to theological seminary, to Basic Youth Conflicts Advanced Seminar, been through the Topical Memory System, and heard the greatest Bible teachers, but if you don't know how to worship, you haven't yet reached that for which you were made. I really mean that! The Christian "experts" come to the Bible as an answer book, rather than a book to get them to God.

Some Christians may be poor in worship simply because they're young in the Lord. They haven't yet learned this great and wonderful task of worship. They don't yet know how to press in, press in to the very heart of God and meet Him there. They've come out of a culture that says, "You go to church on Sunday? Man, don't you have any fun?"

You see, the world is man-centered. It shoots down the idea of what worship is about. And what happens, many times, is that we let the surrounding culture set the mood for us. We mustn't do that. That makes us "worldly" Christians.

On vacation I get to visit as a worshiper in other churches. Most evangelical churches haven't the foggiest idea of worship. It's completely dull and boring to sing hymns when no one seems to be thinking. And who can really pray with a leader who rattles off one cliché after another? We must learn to worship, or church is a terrible drag.

So I say that you've got to think about worship. Then you've got to determine that you are going to do it.

There's a lot of talk today about sitting in rows—how "out of it" that really is. You come to church and sit in these rigid rows, and a person on an elevated place speaks. Terrible! So we think that sitting in a circle somehow gets it done. The big thing is to "share" and "discuss." But that kind of thinking is confusing worship with fellowship. Fellowship is talking with each other. Worship is getting to God. Worship is sitting shoulder to shoulder, eyes "front and center" on God! Worship is for God. Worship is to God.

People say rows are so impersonal. That's right! Jesus took His best friends up the mountain with Him. But then He *withdrew from them a stone's throw* and fell on His face. When you go to worship, meet God personally. Whatever anyone else does around you, you get through to Him.

Notice in John 4 two phrases: in verse 23, "True worshipers shall worship the Father in spirit and truth"; then 24, "Those who worship Him must worship in spirit and truth." Twice that formula "spirit and truth" is given. And it says worship is not something we do if we like, but it says *"shall"* and *"must!"* There are few "musts" in the Bible. Worship is one of them.

Think about it: how do you worship in spirit? That is, how do you worship in the Holy Spirit and in your human spirit as well?

First, it's the Holy Spirit who prompts us to praise correctly. Ephesians 2:18 in *The Living Bible* says, "Now all of us . . . come to God the Father with the Holy Spirit's help because of what Christ has done for us." The whole Trinity is involved. We get to God on the merits of our Lord Jesus, Saviour, present Master in our lives, and we are helped to do this by the energy and understanding of the Holy Spirit. We worship "in the Spirit."

Oh, how we must have the help of the Holy Spirit if we're going to worship! There is a powerful downward drag inside us, because by nature we are not

God-centered, but self-centered. We need that old prayer from the *Book of Common Worship:*

"Almighty God, unto Whom all hearts be open, all desires known, and from Whom no secrets are hid;

Cleanse the thoughts of our hearts, by the inspiration of Thy Holy Spirit,

That we may perfectly love Thee, and worthily magnify Thy Holy Name;

Through Jesus Christ our Lord."

It's the only way.

Your worship, then, must be by the Holy Spirit.

The externals are not important. How often we get "hung up" on externals. The last congregation I was privileged to serve wouldn't permit candles in the church—not for anything! But they wanted their minister in a robe. So, of course, I was happy to wear one. Then I was called to this present pastorate where the evangelical doctrine is identical, and the people love to use candles, but wouldn't think of having their minister wear a robe. And I think God looks down and says, "My dear people, so what!"

The number one ingredient for worship is internal: we must know Christ, for no man calls Jesus "Lord" but by the Holy Spirit (2 Cor. 12:3). And in knowing Christ, we can be led by the Spirit beyond that initial step into the act of worship.

I believe that when John 4 says "they that worship Him must worship Him in spirit," it also means in our spirits, in our own right attitude toward God, in our enthusiasm for God. You can't come to worship

41

to survey the situation, to "see how things are going today." No, no! You will never get to God that way. Let me tell you, it's devastating for a choir to sing to people who are just leaning back, looking over the situation, saying, "Bless me! I dare you!" It kills the spirit. It dampens hearts. I tell you, it hurts everybody.

Watchman Nee, that great Chinese Christian, wrote:

"They cannot be passive in the Body; they dare not merely stand by looking on. For none are so hurtful as onlookers.

"Whether or not we take a public part in things is immaterial; we must always be giving life, so that our absence is felt.

"We cannot say, 'I don't count.' We dare not attend meetings merely as passengers, while others do the work.

"We are His Body, and members in particular, and it is when all the members fulfill their ministry that the life flows."[7]

And, oh, how God is continually reaching for us in the worship service! If only we understood this. Listen to Moffatt's translation of God's words in Isaiah 65:1:

"Ready was I to answer men who never asked me, ready to be found by men who never sought me. I cried out, 'Here am I,' to folk who never called to me." But when His Spirit in grace gets to us, and our limited helplessness nevertheless reaches up to Him—oh, my friend—the sparks of love and worship fly.

Think a minute about the story of the Magi in

42

Matthew 2. They were the first Gentiles ever to come to know Christ. Here they came, seeking Him. They didn't have the Scriptures. They knew very little about spiritual things. But they knew enough to make them come a long distance, probably from as far east as Afghanistan, the center of astrology at that time, all the way to the Holy Land. It took them a long time. (Friend, you don't need to know very much to get to God. Just so you know enough to get to Him.)

Matthew 2:1 and 2:

"Now, after Jesus was born in Bethlehem of Judea, in the days of Herod the king, behold, Magi from the East arrived in Jerusalem, saying, 'Where is He Who has been born King of the Jews? For we saw His star in the East, *and have come to worship Him.*'" (*NASB*)

They're not saying they've come to study this unusual situation. They've come to worship Him! That touches me. And how they did, too, when they found Him.

"They fell down and worshiped Him; and opening their treasures they presented to Him gifts of gold and frankincense and myrrh." (Matt. 2:11, *NASB*). They fell down!

Have you ever prayed actually on your face in humility before God? That's the point of falling down. "I want to be low before God even in my physical position." It would be a good experience for you. Just stretch out on the floor and cry to God.

The Scriptures say that those who know the very most about God—the angels and the archangels in heaven—continually fall down and worship Him. They are on their faces before God. And John, who had leaned on Jesus' chest and had been His best friend, when he was transported into the world above and saw the risen, glorious Christ, fell down as dead before Him. How can we lean back in church and fold our arms?

These Magi learned to worship right away. Their hearts were sensitive. They fell down and worshiped Him, and then they gave Him gifts—beautiful, expensive gifts.

The Word says when they left they "rejoiced with exceeding great joy." When you go to church, how can you tell if you've met Jesus and worshiped Him? If when you leave you're rejoicing.

Now let's think about Monday to Saturday. Our Sunday attitudes are so important. This doesn't mean we have to be perfect; we are sinners as we come to worship—all of us, obviously. And God loves us. But we cannot live a double life. Amos puts the finger on this as God speaks through him in Amos 5:21–24:

"I hate your show and pretense, your hypocrisy of honoring me with your religious feasts and solemn assemblies. I will not accept your burnt offerings and thank offerings. I will not look at your offerings of peace.

"Away with your hymns of praise—they are noise to my ears. I will not listen to your music, no matter how lovely it is.

"I want to see a mighty flood of justice—a torrent of doing good!" (*TLB*).

He amplifies what He means when He goes on in the eighth chapter:

"Listen, you merchants who rob the poor, trampling on the needy;

"You who long for the Sabbath to end and the religious holidays to be over, so you can get out and start cheating again—using your weighted scales and your under-sized measures;

"You who make slaves of the poor, buying them for their debt of a piece of silver or a pair of shoes, or selling them your moldy wheat—

"The Lord, the Pride of Israel, has sworn: 'I won't forget your deeds!' " (Amos 8:4-7, *TLB*).

If you really plan to worship, you'll discover your whole life will be changed. What happens? You worship, and God purges your life with holy fire. You come out of a worship service saying, "I'll never play football like that," or "I'll never treat people like that again." You come out into a new way of life. Then back you go into another time of cleansing worship before God with the people of God. Worship burns out sin. When God's people learn real corporate worship, then He is like a consuming fire among them. Kids at school will say, "I like being friends with the people from that church."

"Worship in spirit," says John 4, but also, "worship in truth." Two times Jesus says, "Worship in truth." I believe that means you have to involve your mind in worship.

We live in a very sensuous day. We think we're intellectual, but actually our moods, our feelings determine much that we think or do.

Years ago an automobile tire was advertised by describing the quality of the tire. Today it's sold, really, by showing a girl in a bikini standing by the tire! What's the relationship? There is none. It's just a sensuous ad. The ad-men hope that somehow by association, when you see that tire you'll subtly *feel* good, and you'll buy one.

Years ago Folger's Coffee used to be advertised by sound facts. It was grown in South America, it was roasted in a certain way, it was carefully packaged and that made it better than other coffees. Now how does Folger's Coffee advertise? Like this: "Folger's . . . Aaahh!"

Today we can easily get caught using a certain tone of voice—"Jesus . . ." and saying, "Oh-h-h, that's really worshipful!" Not necessarily! Who is this Jesus, whose name you're repeating? What are your doctrinal facts about Him? What do you mean when you say, "Jesus"? You must worship Him in truth! Is He the lovely, risen, exalted, coming again, Son of the Living God? We must engage our minds.

A critic once said, "When I go to church I feel like unscrewing my head and placing it under the seat, because in a religious meeting I never have any use for anything above my collar button." Now, I'm sorry for him, because if he were at all coming to meet God, he'd have lots to use above his collar button. But I think what he's saying is, "I don't like a strictly emotional type of worship in which my mind is not fully engaged."

God is a rational God. He calls on us to come to Him with minds as well as hearts. "I beseech you therefore, brethren, by the mercies of God that you present your bodies," your faculties, "unto God which is your reasonable service" (Rom. 12:1).

Heaven's population knows all about Christ. And their real view of God is true. Their real view of

God is full-orbed, and so their enthusiasm is also intelligent! Heaven worships Him best.

Revelation 19 tells of that wonderful scene around the throne of God in heaven:

"And the twenty-four elders and the four living creatures fell down and worshiped God, who sits on the throne, saying, 'Amen! Hallelujah!' " (v. 4, *NASB*). (Oh, the great fervor, the heartiness! We need this, too, don't we?)

"The voice" (out of heaven came) "of a great multitude and as the sound of many waters and as the sound of mighty peals of thunder, saying, 'Hallelujah! For the Lord our God, the Almighty reigns. Let us rejoice and be glad and give the glory to Him . . .'" (v. 6, *NASB*). You see, when we know much, we worship and magnify Him much.

Giving your attention to God takes all the concentration you can muster. We evangelicals haven't thought enough about these things. For instance, you need to get ready to worship. Perhaps you should come early, maybe even a half-hour, and just sit before God. Or instead of coming in, maybe you need to take a five-minute walk outside, thinking of God, talking to Him. You need to "wind down," don't you?—so that you can get into worship and "wind up" the right way! You need to learn how to pray and love God before the service.

Friend, you have an appointment with God Almighty, the King of kings, and no cup of coffee, no conversation with any friend should make you late to that appointment. You have an audience with Him. If He sovereignly allows you to have a flat tire on the way, then praise Him as you change it! But pray for yourself as you come in, and pray for others, and pray for those who participate from the pulpit and choir.

Then when you come into church, put blinders on! And help others to wear blinders! Don't move around. Don't be distracting. Don't talk. Slip quietly into church and go to God. Give your whole mind and heart to Him.

At the very first happening of the service, engage your mind. Get with God. Get with the people of God. Sing! Think when you sing, and sing to God. When the choir sings—my, don't read the bulletin! Put that aside; read it when you go home. Let the choir speak to you for God, and speak to God for you. I beg you in Jesus' name, learn how to worship as others lift you up. The music is merely the vehicle to make the words really come home strong.

When the Bible is read, do as that hymn says, "Beyond the sacred page, I see Thee, Lord."

When prayer is offered, be with God. He is never dull or boring! Pray for those who pray, that they will prepare and think before they come and be in the Spirit as they pray. It's an awesome thing to lead a company of people in prayer.

During the sermon, take notes. Underline in your Bible. Make some notes to yourself—"This I want to do. . . ." Remember that Paul said to the Corinthian church, "The preaching of the cross is to them that perish foolishness, but to us who are saved, it is the power of God." The New Testament shows that the sermon is the whole congregation declaring their faith together. Forsythe, the great preacher, said, "It is the organized hallelujah of the whole church!"

Leading in worship and preaching is terrifying! It needs the support of much prayer.

At the end of the service, seal it all up and then plan by God's grace to go and *do* the truth.

Now, it's important to remember this: we don't want to be worship-centered; we want to be God-centered! We don't want to go out exclaiming, "Wasn't that some kind of worship!" No, "Wasn't it great to meet God!" You can fall off a horse either way, you know. That would be like being in love with love, instead of being in love with a lover.

We want to worship God, to be with Him. Go with your brothers and sisters, with all of your hearts, to God together. The words "in the spirit and in truth" mean "in the atmosphere of Spirit,"—of the Holy Spirit; and in the atmosphere of truth—the truth of Christ.

Worship is elevating. It's healing. It's comforting. It's enriching. It's Christ-honoring. It's a growing thing to worship God.

I challenge you to learn how.

1. Read Psalms 95 and 100. If you had had this attitude of joy, how would your last public worship experience have been different?

2. How can you make your next worship experience better? Review this chapter just before you publicly worship again. Afterwards check and see how many of the suggestions you put into practice.

3. Write out what it means to you to worship God. Then talk over your definition with Him.

COMMITMENT 2

Commit yourself to the body of Christ.

The little plane jostled over air pockets high over South American mountain peaks, and four of us looked in each others' eyes; Cliff, Carl, my wife Anne, and I. Then we prayed together above the roar of the motor.

"Lord, here we are. You're sending us to minister to these Wycliffe missionaries of Colombia and Panama. We know almost none of them, but we believe in Your strategy. You're going to bring us together for a reason. . . ."

I'd been asked to be speaker at the annual business and inspiration get-together of this Wycliffe branch, but because of Commitment Number Two, we're learning at Lake Avenue not to move in solo motions. We minister in teams. We make decisions with the brothers. We "get sent" or we don't "go."

So I'd answered Wycliffe as I do all speaking invitations, "Look, I'll come if I can bring a team. From somewhere God will scare up the money. . . ."

"Ah—okay," came the answer, and we prayed as the Spirit chose Anne (her plane fare was offered out of the blue), and Cliff and Carl, a school principal and a dentist who arranged to be released from their work.

The four of us already knew and loved each other

well. But as usual, in preparation God ground us by mortar and pestle until we were one stuff.

Wasn't it always true with Paul and his teams? Of Barnabas, Silas, Timothy, Titus, etc., Paul wrote, "For we have the same Holy Spirit, and walk in each other's steps, doing things the same way" (2 Cor. 12:18, *TLB*).

So the little plane descended into Loma Linda, a clearing in the jungle—Honda City, Carl named it. We four met once a day to report, pray, plan, laugh, cry, and beseech God. Otherwise we scattered, multiplying ourselves: four mouths with one message.

In the meetings any or all of us might speak. We were the Body at work. Commitment Number Two in three dimensions.

Then we discovered what we were there for. Dear missionaries! How wonderful they were.

Obviously they were committed to Number One—God, or they would never have trained to become highly skilled linguists and then turn their backs on well-paying American jobs to translate the Bible from unknown tongues.

Obviously they were committed to Number Three—their work, or they would never have slogged their way to some of the world's most primitive areas to spend years putting strange grunts and groans on paper.

But commitment to the Body? They had jumped from One to Three, and they were lonely even in their togetherness.

We told them how we were learning to do it in the Company of the Committed. In small groups—"I'm responsible for you, and you're responsible for me . . . Everything I have is yours; use me . . . I'll agonize over your kids, and you agonize over mine . . . Teach me what you know in the Word, and I'll teach you what I know . . . Here's where I'm weak; hold me accountable, and pray me to strength . . . Let's learn together to worship God. . . ."

For these very committed, zealous, work-oriented accomplishers, the cry was, "How do I have time for this? I can hardly get my work done now. . . ."

Four work-pressed Pasadenans' freshly out of the great Southern California pace said, "Then you postpone your goals. The Body comes first—your wife, your children, your lonely neighbor, your hurting friend. . . ."

On the eighth day, Thursday morning at an eight o'clock meeting, the Wycliffe branch of Colombia-Panama melted into a working part of the body of Christ. (Somebody chuckled afterward, "I always thought revival could only happen at night!")

Christians expressed their love for each other. They apologized for past hurts. Tears and laughter ebbed and flowed as they poured out what they'd been holding inside for a long time. They prayed for each other on the spot. Very real and human fears of the jungle melted away. Genuine compassion and love for the Indian tribes was kindled. Believers sought out believers and automatically became small groups.

I just heard the other day of a tape from one of them, reporting eighteen months later how life-changing that week was for him.

Christian, the priorities cannot be three, one. They can't be one, three. They've got to be one, two, three.

In that order.

5

PUT IT TOGETHER WITH OTHER BELIEVERS

A kid who went off to college for the first time wrote, "Mom, I'm so lonesome. Deep down inside I feel so unsure of myself."

An older friend said to me recently, "I've known a sense of aloneness all my life, but never more keenly than now. My children are nice to me. I know they love me. But I'm a problem to them. I'd like to talk to them, share my heart, but when I try, I can see that they don't understand."

We all know loneliness. Christ comes to deal with this sense of aloneness by bringing us into fellowship with Him and His church. Many an older Christian, and many a younger one coming out of non-Christian backgrounds, have said to me, "You know, I feel closer to the people of this church than I feel to my own family. Here they truly understand me."

The greatest resource that you and I have is the presence of Jesus Christ Himself. The second most precious possession is the fellowship of God's people.

I want us to look at three basic Scriptures that have to do with fellowship—relationships in the family of God. One is from Matthew, one from Malachi, one from Romans.

Matthew speaks of the promised presence of Christ. Malachi speaks of the attitude of God towards those who gather together to worship Him. And Paul gives the spiritual ingredients of Christian friendship and fellowship.

So let's go to these. Matthew 18:20 records words spoken by Jesus:

"For where two or three are gathered together in my name, there am I in the midst of them."

Christ loves the gathering of those who love Him. Even the smallest number is important to Him! He knows, you see, the tragedy of spiritual aloneness. He knows the failure of the Christian who lives in voluntary solitary confinement. To be alone (unless it is ordained of God, when one is thrust into this because of some special situation), to choose to be alone, is to invite sure failure.

Remember in the Old Testament the Jews were instructed by Moses' law to gather together several times a year. They came from far and near, from all over, to Jerusalem to celebrate. Sometimes they came to eat for a whole week; sometimes to weep together; sometimes to rejoice in all that God had done; sometimes to sorrow. But these huge gatherings of God's people were so important, because by their gathering together, *God knew that they would maintain*

their identity as His chosen people. "Where two or
three are gathered together in My name, there am
I . . . !"

The Psalmist talks about the gathering of Israel.
David says, "We took sweet counsel together, and
walked unto the house of God in company" (Ps.
55:14). Isn't that beautiful? That's why Hebrews says,
"Forsake not the assembling of ourselves together
as the manner of some is . . ." but as Christ's coming
is approaching, watch that church attendance! Or as
Phillips puts it, "Let us not hold aloof from church
meetings, as some do."

But Sunday church services, wonderful as they are,
aren't enough. Catch the flavor of the lifestyle of the
early Christians. Acts 2:44–46 tells how they met
together constantly, daily—in two ways: they worshiped together regularly in the Temple, everybody
all at once; and they broke bread together daily in
small groups in each other's homes.

Not either/or, my friend, but both. The church
service will be cold if you come together as strangers.
(And believe me, I mean strangers who have known
each other for years!) But when you've been together
constantly in small groups, studying, praying, con-
fessing your needs, holding each other accountable,
lifting each other up, then you'll be drawn together
on Sunday into the magnetic field of Holy Spirit-filled
love and praise!

Back again to these small groups. Jesus says,
"Where two or three are gathered *in My name* . . ."
The basis of our special friendship is the name of
Christ. We are people of the Name. Someone said,
"Every man is like the company he keeps." Or, "Tell

57

me thy company, and I will tell thee what thou art." Thomas Carlyle said, "Show me the man you honor, and by that, better than any other, I know what kind of a man you are." The wise Solomon writes in the Old Testament, Proverbs 13:20: "He that walketh with wise men shall be wise: but a companion of fools shall be destroyed."

You see, ultimately we all choose our friends. Be sure to choose them carefully!

Your friendships are your responsibilities. And if your friendships are in Christ, you'll find in these deep gatherings together, that something happens to you. You become an imitator of the people you're with.

We're all like that white "boring shell" that's found at the beach. If it attaches itself to a brown rock, it becomes brown; or a red rock, it becomes red. We become like the people with whom we associate. We will become like Christ and like His people as He is among us.

Turn to Malachi 3:16. Christ not only promises to meet with those who meet with others in His name, but also He records what we talk about when we meet together!

"Then those who feared the Lord spoke with one another; the Lord heeded and heard them, and a book of remembrance was written before him of those who feared the Lord and thought of his name." (*RSV*) Note that the King James version says "spoke often with one another," but I think that weakens it a bit. The word "often" was not in the original. This was not a "now again, then again" happening; this was a way of life! His people were continually talking about God together.

This talking together has to be a structured thing. Otherwise, even though our intentions are good, our lives are too cluttered and it gets crowded out.

My wife Ann wears a bracelet given to her by her three special Christian sisters. It has three charms on it, each one engraved with a name and a particular Bible verse. Let me describe to you how these four "spoke with one another" for one particular twelve-month period. Every Tuesday and Thursday morning each phoned each of the other three. Each sister knew she was to be ready with something to share from the Scriptures—something fresh since the last telephone call. Then the last few days would be reviewed. Needs would be prayed for over the telephone. Praise would be offered for successes. The days' schedules until next contact time would be projected and prayed over. Then every other Wednesday noon the four met for lunch, and this meeting was primarily for praise, adoration and worship.

This kind of structured "speaking together" in small groups is duplicated hundreds of times over each week in the life of the church.

Notice Malachi says that God "heeded them." He noticed them right away. He bent over and listened, and He wrote down what they said. God watches carefully that we fulfill our human responsibility of sharing our hearts with other people. God's attitude towards fellowship is that wherever there is fellowship, He comes!

Of course, why wouldn't this be true? Our God

is a togetherness God. He is Father, Son, and Holy Spirit. He's not a single unit, an isolated loner. Our God is *in Himself* fellowship, and we who are made in His image were not made to be loners—to make our decisions all by ourselves, to hoard our resources for ourselves, to turn inward, to be a solitary figure among other solitary figures.

The word "fellowship" is an interesting one. It comes from an Anglo-Saxon word which is really "fee"-lowship. The word "fee" meant cow, and cows in those days were a man's wealth! (We still use the word "fee" today for a payment of money.)

So when people really trusted each other, they established a joint bank account—they put their cows together. The walls were broken down, the fences removed; they could put their cows together. They'd say, "I want to have fellowship with you. I trust you."

This is how God calls us together. I have a deep suspicion that we twentieth-century believers have much to learn from the early Christians' pooling their funds. We haven't even begun to take seriously yet what deep fellowship can mean.

Billy Graham, when asked what he would do if he pastored a church today, said:

"I think one of the first things I would do would be to get a small group of eight or ten or twelve men around me who would meet a few hours a week and pay the price! It would cost them something in time and effort. I would share with them everything I have, over a period of a couple of years. Then I would actually have twelve ministers among the laymen, who in turn could take eight or ten or twelve more and teach them."[1]

Christ Himself has set the pattern. He spent most of His time with twelve—with eternal results. He called the twelve that they might be with Him. He worked with them, trained them and loved them, and He let them train each other. There was a cross-current of the work of God's Spirit as these disciples were together.

Discipling is as crucial a need as there is among believers today. Every Christian needs some older Christian he's learning from, and some younger Christian he's teaching. It's the function of the whole Body to do this.

Believer, whom do you know who could disciple you? Pray over it and then go ask if he feels led to take you on. Be willing to pay the price of submission. But don't forget that Ephesians 5 says submission is required of *all* of us, as we're filled with the Holy Spirit.

And then, whom should you disciple? Don't just pour your life into anybody. If they're too involved in this world, they'll probably always just follow Jesus afar off. But look for these qualifications:

1. Heart
2. Teachability
3. Availability

This is obedience to the last command Christ ever gave us: "Go ye into all the world and make disciples . . . teaching them to observe all things whatsoever I have commanded you."

This is gutsy, biblical Christianity!

Paul did this. He never went out alone. You notice it's always Paul and Sosthenes and Timothy writing to the churches. Turn to the last part of Romans and you see it isn't just Paul alone. He travels with a band of men, and he's committed to men who are committed to him. He says, verses 21 and 22, chapter 16 of Romans, "Timothy, my fellow worker, greets you." Why? Because Timothy is one of his travelers, one of those who is with him, one of the "cell group," a partner in the gospel. He says, "So do Lucius and Jason and Sosipater, my kinsmen. I Tertius. . . ." (Their secretary sends his greetings.) And then Romans 16:23, "Gaius, who is host to me and to the whole church, greets you." Paul never flew solo!

God works great things in His gathered people. There were a few men who were meeting for prayer at Williams College in Massachusetts many years ago. One day as they were meeting for prayer, praying about world needs, a storm came up and they took refuge under the overhanging shelf of a haystack. And there under the haystack, God met them in such a great way that they began what we know today as the modern missionary movement. Those men fanned out all over the world. It was God meeting them as they were committed to each other, and to the gospel together; and God guided and directed them.

One Episcopal minister writes from Trinity Episcopal Church, on Wall Street in New York,

"It is a growing conviction of mine that no parish can fulfill its true function unless there is at the very center of its leadership life a small community of quietly fanatic, changed and truly converted Christians.

"The trouble with most parishes is that nobody,

including the rector, is really greatly changed; but even where there is a devoted, self-sacrificing priest at the heart of the fellowship, not much will happen until there is a community of changed men and women."[2]

This happens as men and women draw their hearts together for prayer, for study of the Word, and in communion and fellowship together.

Just for a few moments turn to Romans chapter 15, and get some guidelines for fellowship.

First, Paul tells us to make our fellowships broad. Don't just gather around you people who think as you think. Romans 15:1-3 says:

"We who are strong ought to bear with the failings of the weak, and not to please ourselves; let each of us please his neighbor for his good, to edify him. For Christ did not please Himself . . ." (*RSV*)

In your friendships, include weak people. You may ask, "Well, who are the weak?" Look at chapter 14, verses 1 and 2:

"As for the man who is weak in faith, welcome him, but not for disputes over opinions. One believes he may eat anything, while *the weak man eats only vegetables.*" (*RSV*)

The weak man is the legalist, the one who gets his security out of not doing this and doing that. Paul says in the next verses, "Now don't despise this man. Receive him. Love him. Do not be narrow and restricted in your fellowship *because you feel he might be.*"

Verse 19 of chapter 14: "Let us then pursue what makes for peace and for mutual upbuilding." Our fellowship can be rich in differences, and prove that none other than the Holy Spirit is the glue that holds us tightly together!

Secondly, make your fellowship genuine. See Romans 15:7:

"Welcome one another, therefore, as Christ has welcomed (or received) you for the glory of God." How did Christ welcome or receive you? Well, He received you with your "hang-ups" and your sins and your problems and your troubles and your immaturity. He received you just as you were. And in the same way we're to come to each other just as we are. We sing a hymn,

> "Just as I am
>   Without one plea,
> But that Thy blood
>   Was shed for me;
> Lamb of God, I come."

Unless we welcome each other just as we are, there will be no place for genuine fellowship. The Word breaks down isolation; and receiving and welcoming one another breaks down barriers.

Proverbs 27:19 says, "As in water face answers face, so the heart of man to man." This is the way we are to be together—open, reflecting what we really are to each other.

James 5:16 tells us to confess our faults to each other so that we may be healed. This is possible where people have been working close together and they finally find that they can be absolutely open because they're loved. I don't think there ought to be brutal frankness, where you "mow everybody down" because you say you're being honest. I don't want any kind of fellowship like that. I need to be handled tenderly, and so do you.

Even when we come to church we can be unknown and lonely for years. If your real self, your real thoughts, your real longings are never shared by anyone—that, my friend, is aloneness. God wants to break that down and bring you into Christian fellowship where you're received.

A Congregational minister came into our Wednesday evening prayer meeting recently. We often break into small groups to pray. The people in his group were introducing each other. He said, "I'm an engineer. I'm out here with my company, but on weekends I preach. I've got some concerns, and I'd like you to pray for them." That man could come to a fellowship of Pasadena Christians and just be himself! We all joined with him and his life and his loves and his purposes, and there was fellowship. He prayed for us and our needs. He will go back to Wisconsin feeling truly received by the Christians in Pasadena. "Bear ye one another's burdens," says Galatians 6:2, "and so fulfill the law of Christ."

Make your friendships broad; make them genuine.

Thirdly, the Scripture tells us to make friendships useful, to have a ministry together. It's not just so that we may feel good. You and others must be bound together in purpose. There's a triangle of movement here: for God, for helping each other, and then for ministry. We have to have something that's really important. Fellowship isn't two people looking at each other; it's two people looking away together at something else—at Christ and His purposes.

"Stand firm in one spirit and one mind," says Paul,

"striving side by side for faith in the Gospel" (Phil. 4:27). That's real Christian fellowship and comradeship, and it's so appealing. It's so good, and the world can't possibly deny this.

One evening a group of men were meeting in downtown New York City. They had met sometime together and they had wonderful fellowship, sharing the Word of God and sharing their heart's concerns. A stranger came in. They all thought that someone else had invited him. So he just sat in and listened as they shared about their frustrations and their needs, and as they enjoyed sharing the gospel and loving Christ and reading the Word together. Finally they asked this fellow who he was. He said, "My name is Paul. As long as you have been honest, I'll be honest. I'm a dope addict. I came here to rob you to get a fix. But I think I've found something better."

Yes, fellowship is something infinitely better!

My Christian friend, how are you doing?

1. Begin meeting once a week before school or at lunch with a Christian friend to talk over how it's going at being Christians on campus.

2. Draw a body like this one on a piece of paper. On it write names of Christians you will support this week and what you will do for each person.

3. Read Romans 12:4-21 and 1 Corinthians 12:12-27. List qualities of a healthy, supportive Christian. Check those which describe you and circle two traits you want to further develop.

6
HAVE
A CLOSE FRIEND

When a woman knits, she uses two needles—one in her right hand, and one in her left. As she knits, two pieces of yarn, the left and the right, come together to become one solid fabric.

First Samuel 18:1 says that "The soul of Jonathan was knit to the soul of David, and Jonathan loved him as his own soul."

You were made to so knit your life with others, that together you weave a beautiful fabric for the glory of God.

Let me share my heart with you about friendship—friendships that last forever. Not friendliness; everyone should be friendly to everyone else. But I'm talking about establishing selective, godly friendships. Let's look at the story of Jonathan and David:

how their friendship began, how it developed, and how it continued.

Start with 1 Samuel 14 and meet Jonathan. Goliath had begun coming down and challenging the Israelites for battle between him and whoever they might choose. Young, unknown David defeated Goliath and won the day—and won Jonathan's admiration. But a few weeks before that, Jonathan had had quite a day all by himself.

The Philistines were making raids on the Israelites. They were strong, they were threatening, and the whole safety of Israel was at stake. Every able Israelite was out in the hills and valleys in defense—even the king's son, Jonathan.

"Jonathan said to the young man who bore his armor, 'Come, let us go over to the garrison of these uncircumcised; it may be that the Lord will work for us; for nothing can hinder the Lord from saving, by many or by few' " (1 Sam. 14:6, *RSV*).

Isn't that great? Jonathan says to his armor-bearer, "Naturally the Lord is going to win the battle, whether by many or by few. Hey, just for fun, let's see if He does it by few?—like two?"

We're seeing several exciting things about Jonathan: of course, his spirit—that he was bold for God, full of faith and courage. But also that before he ever met David, he knew how to make deep friendships. Between him and his armor-bearer there was commitment of heart to heart.

"And his armor-bearer said to him, 'Do all that your mind inclines to; behold, I am with you; as is your mind, so is mine.' " (v. 7) "Jonathan," he says,

"I'm yours. You say the word and we'll go." These two young believers were absolutely counting on God.

"And they fell before Jonathan!"

As a result, all Israel loved Jonathan; and when there came a problem between Jonathan and his father Saul, all the people rose up and said, "Don't touch a hair of Jonathan's head." He was a real hero.

Such a man as Jonathan—why do you suppose he allowed Goliath to come up those forty days and taunt Israel? Having gone through such experiences, why would he let one man shake the cage of Israel so badly? I don't really know, and I suppose nobody does, because we're not told. But maybe Jonathan comes back after this tremendous rout of the enemy, and he sees all these weak-kneed, unbelieving people, and he sees his father the king slipping back into his old depressions, disobeying God and losing control of the people—and Jonathan might have said, "What's the use? Nobody cares."

But when he saw David walk out of that valley with Goliath's head in his hand—David, just a shepherd boy, a slight lad, younger than Jonathan himself—I can imagine that a man with a heart like Jonathan said, "How about that? How about that? There's my man! What a man!" Or something like that. Jonathan loved manliness, and David was a man.

I don't know about you, but I desperately need men around me who are giant-killers. I have an innate tendency to fear; I need fearless, godly men. The story of many a Christian is that he starts warm with God—"Take it all, Lord. You can have anything I have." As a result God blesses him and pretty soon he "has it made." Then he wants to "keep it made" and protect himself, and no longer get out where he's depending wholly on God. I fear this! Oh, how I fear this.

We simply have to be out on the cutting edge, my friend, or there's enough sin in every one of us that after awhile we'll just be "zeros." That's why a godly friend or two is utterly essential. They must be friends who are courageous enough to exhort and rebuke us, as well as encourage us.

With all our emphasis these days on the Body, I think we have hardly even discovered the possibility of what a Spirit-given, committed friend can do in our lives.

One of the young men of our church said to me ten days ago, "I don't know whether my brothers in Christ are really committed to me or not. A month ago I shared with them three goals I'd like to reach: to establish a consistent daily quiet time, to stick to a diet that will take off fifteen pounds, and to adhere rigidly to a new budget that will discipline my wife and me not to overspend."

He looked at me earnestly. "I can't make it without these guys. But since I told them about these goals four weeks ago, not one of them has asked me how I'm doing. Not one has checked up on me."

"Tell them!" I said. "They're responsible for you! If they've committed their hearts to you, your failure is their failure. You're all in this together."

The next morning was their weekly breakfast together. My young friend laid it on the table. "Do

70

you guys love me, or don't you? Do you care, or not?"

I saw him again yesterday. He grinned, "Man, those guys were smitten. Almost every day since, somebody's called me—hey, you sticking to your diet? You had your quiet time yet today? No impulse buying, Buddy. . . ."

There was great confidence in his eyes. "I'll make it," he said. My answer was, "Their need to keep responsible for you is just as great as your need to keep accountable to them."

I want you to see how this friendship of Jonathan and David developed. Chapter 18 says that "the soul of Jonathan was knit to the soul of David, and Jonathan loved him as his own soul." It takes time to knit something; the process calls for skill and care. Then if we're going to have friendships in which our hearts are knit together with others, we must carefully select people that God gives us who will join their hearts with ours.

There are many people I'd love to have my heart knit together with, but knitting takes time. So the point is to look for those people whom because of circumstances I'm naturally thrown in with. God says to us by the very example of Jonathan and David, "Listen, become deep friends with someone, or with two, three, or four."

Someone may ask, "How many can it be?" I don't know what your capacity for loving is. Paul knit his heart together with many people. In Colossians 2 he prayed that Christians' hearts might be knit together in love, because he had experienced this. Everywhere

Paul went, he had a young brother with him. As he wrote to this church and that place, he told how dearly he loved them: how Epaphroditus was willing to lay down his life for him, and how Timothy encouraged him in the Lord. The body of Christ today must be knit together in the same way.

Wherever you are, Christian, because of your place in life, you can be close to some other believer. Have you someone that your heart is knit to? Are there several to whom you've so committed yourself, that you are theirs and they are yours?

Shakespeare's Hamlet says of his special friends, "Grapple them to thy soul with hoops of steel!"

Jesus, in the days of His flesh, had the three very special friends. Then He had the twelve—very close. He poured His time into them. Then He had the seventy whom He trained and sent forth. Then there were the hundred and twenty. He loved them all alike, in a sense. Yet He was particularly woven into the fabric of the lives of some who were very special.

Today, of course, Jesus is risen, ascended, and is no longer limited physically or geographically. Now He can say to each one of us, "I will never leave you, nor forsake you. I will be with you." The miracle of the resurrected, omnipresent One is that He is knit to us as the closest Friend of all. As bone is knit to bone, so is the Head perfectly fused to the Body.

But the way we learn to express our love for the Head is the way we learn to express our love for somebody who is flesh and blood—with all the nitty-gritty working-out of love that that involves!

David and Jonathan's friendship was not just a

pink cloud of emotion. It began with a verbal agreement:

"Then Jonathan made a covenant with David, because he loved him as his own soul. And Jonathan stripped himself of the robe that was upon him, and gave it to David, and his armor, and even his sword and his bow and his girdle" (1 Sam. 18:3,4, *RSV*).

This was a tremendously symbolic thing. Remember that Jonathan was heir-apparent to the throne—he was Saul's son. David was his subject. But Jonathan loved him so, he took off his special robe and gave it to David. He took off the belt in which he had his wealth, and he gave that to David. He is saying in this way, "All I have is yours, David. Everything I have."

Listen, have you ever said that to anybody? No? Then you haven't lived. You need to say to somebody, "Everything I have is yours." It's easy to be a loner, to protect yourself for yourself. There are lots of evangelical loners! They really do love Jesus, but they don't love His church too much. It's incongruous, and it's sin. Real fellowship calls for gutsy commitment.

Christ Himself initiates this kind of friendship. He says to you, "Everything I have is yours. All My righteousness I give to you." The "riches of His glory by Christ Jesus" are yours. And He says, "Now, you give Me everything of yours in return." You say, "All right, Lord, I give You my sins, I give You my failures, I give You my inabilities. . . ." And He says, "Fine, fine! That's a deal." Then He gives you forgiveness, constant love, friendship. Beautiful!

When we've done that, we're ready for godly

friendships with each other. How we Christians of today need to learn the fulness of the Christian life! This isn't *all* the Christian life, but it is a very important part—to strip ourselves for each other, my friend. To strip ourselves.

We don't know this yet. God is working to teach us. I was meeting weekly with a small group of seminary students. What quality young men! And how they had given their hearts to each other.

But one afternoon as we met together, one of them was totally discouraged. "I just can't make it financially, with Joanie and the baby," he said. "I've got to drop out of seminary."

One of the other fellow's eyes filled with tears, "Ted," he said (I'm using fictitious names), "I never want to hear you say that again. You're a good student, and obviously God wants you to finish. As long as you're in school, whenever you need money, I'll supply it. Just let me know. I don't ever again want to hear you talk of quitting because of finances."

You're probably thinking this fellow had money. He didn't. He was also going through seminary with a wife and baby, and he was as poor as Ted. He just happened to have more faith in that particular area. It was a holy moment.

I never heard whether Ted ever asked John for money. I only know that both Ted and John knew the offer was absolutely valid. And I know that Ted finished seminary—on schedule, with a good academic record.

There's an exquisite scene in 1 Samuel 20:42, look at it. Remember that David had to hide from Saul because Saul was so jealous. And now Jonathan and David are meeting alone.

"Then Jonathan said to David, 'Go in peace, forasmuch as we have sworn both of us in the name of the Lord . . .' " (*RSV*)

What did they swear to each other? Listen: "The Lord shall be between me and you." They were bound together in God. The Lord was the cohesive factor. I want you to see how deep and long-standing their friendship was to be. Jonathan continues: "And the Lord be between my descendants and your descendants forever."

That's saying, "I will love your kids; and my kids will love your kids; and my kids' kids are going to love your kids' kids!" I can hardly imagine anything more marvelous than this. How deep their friendship was to go! They not only bound their lives together, but they bound their children's lives together, and their children's children's lives after that.

In 1 Samuel 23 we see that last time these two friends will ever meet. They don't know it, but very soon Jonathan is going to be killed in battle.

"David was afraid because Saul had come out to seek his life. David was in the Wilderness of Ziph at Horesh.

"And Jonathan, Saul's son, rose, and went to David at Horesh, and strengthened his hand in God" (vv. 15,16, *RSV*). "David was afraid." This is where a friend must come in. Jonathan finds him and says, "Oh, David, don't ever forget that God has anointed you. David, take heart." He "strengthened his hand in God."

"He said to him, 'Fear not; for the hand of Saul my father shall not find you; you shall be king over Israel, and I shall be next to you; Saul my father also knows this'" (v. 17).

What an amazing thing for Jonathan to say—Jonathan, physically next in line to the throne. "David, my joy is that you will be the king, and if I can just stand next to you, that will be enough."

Friend, do you know how to support your friend in God? Gals, do you ever strengthen your brother's hand in God? Fellows, do you ever strengthen your sister in God? Or you young men whose hearts are bound together, do you strengthen each other with the Word of God and with encouragement? Do you know how to give this?

"You know Timothy's worth," wrote Paul, "how as a son with a father, he has served me in the gospel."

Some of us men were sitting around a conference table at our church. What had begun as a committee had become a band of men. God had knit our hearts together. And now we were pledging ourselves to one another. None of us will ever forget it. One was discouraged—dear, dear friend. He said, "I don't know if I can commit myself to you. I'm so discouraged, I feel so weak, I don't have anything to offer to you guys." And one of the other men said, "All right, this is the time for us to pour our lives into you. There'll come a time later when you can strengthen us."

Jonathan said to David, "I'm stronger now, but soon you will be. You'll be king, and I shall just stand by your side." Gladly Jonathan hands over all the glory of position to David. What wonderful self-lessness! "I shall be next to you."

I wonder if David, after Jonathan died, ever thought, "Oh, Jonathan, man I loved, I feel you next to me. In a different way than you thought, Jonathan, you'll always be next to me!"

Hebrews 12 tells about the "great cloud of witnesses around us." The testimony of all those saints through the years continually surrounds us and encourages us: "Stand firm! Believe God."

Thank You, Lord.

I want my memory to linger with somebody. I want to stand by somebody when I'm gone.

Even after death, the friendship between Jonathan and David continued . . . unbroken. The last chapter of 1 Samuel:

"Now the Philistines fought against Israel; and the men of Israel fled the Philistines, and fell slain on Mount Gilboa.

"And the Philistines overtook Saul and his sons;

"And the Philistines slew Jonathan . . ." (1 Sam. 31:1,2, *RSV*). David hears about it—2 Samuel 1:11,12:

"David took hold of his clothes, and rent them; and so did all the men who were with him; and they mourned and wept and fasted until evening for Saul and for Jonathan his son, and for the people of the Lord, and for the house of Israel, because they had fallen by the sword" (*RSV*).

And then verse 17:

"And David lamented with this lamentation over Saul and Jonathan. . . ."

"Saul and Jonathan!" How beautiful for David to speak so kindly of Saul, who had haunted him and threatened him all of his life! His word was, "Touch not the Lord's anointed." David was a man who just wouldn't speak evil of man. Look at the magnanimous spirit of David:

"Saul and Jonathan," he sings, "beloved and lovely! In life and in death they were not divided."

Verse 25:

"How are the mighty fallen in the midst of battle!

"Jonathan lies slain upon thy high places. I am distressed for you, my brother Jonathan; very pleasant you have been to me; your love to me was wonderful, passing the love of women.

"How are the mighty fallen!"

Friend, do you have a loving circle of friends with whom, when they live, you live; and when they die, in a sense, you die? Do you have friends who will love you and your children, and your children's children? If you don't have anyone like that, step out by faith. Live a little dangerously, and give your heart away. Find someone who will be a godly friend to you, who will strengthen your hand in God. I plead with you for this.

If the only thing you can talk about is what you ate for dinner last, or how classes are going—those things are good to talk about once in awhile, but you've got to get deeper than that. Sometimes you've got to get to the soul! You and God and that person must link your hearts and arms together and say, "We're going to go together. We love each other, and we're going to pray each other through and lift each other up."

About 1638 the Old Scotch Covenanters in Edinburgh went out in a churchyard and drew up a covenant together. They vowed that they would "hang together," and they signed the covenant with the blood of their own veins. That was the beginning of a powerful movement of God in human history.

How true was David to his pledge of commitment? Look at 2 Samuel 4:4:

"Jonathan, the son of Saul, had a son who was crippled in his feet.

"He was about five years old when the news about Saul and Jonathan came from Jezreel; and his nurse took him up, and fled; and, as she fled in her haste, he fell, and became lame.

"And his name was Mephibosheth."

Verse 12 of chapter 5:

"And David perceived that the Lord had established him king over Israel, and that he had exalted his kingdom for the sake of his people Israel." (*RSV*)

Now David had "arrived." He "had it made." Outwardly, he needed no one.

All right, David, how about your pledge to Jonathan about his children? How good is your word?

You remember in the "Song of Norway," that beautiful motion picture, Edvard Grieg's struggle to succeed as a composer. His friend had poured his life into him. And now the friend was dying, and he sent word to Edvard, "Come see me." But Edvard was a big hero now, and there were concerts, receptions . . . he never made it. What a heartbreak! I don't know about you, but I wept.

What about David, now so successful, the darling of the people? 2 Samuel 9:1:

"And David said, 'Is there still any one left of the house of Saul, that I may show him kindness for Jonathan's sake?' " Hooray! Good for you, David!

"Mephibosheth, the son of Jonathan, the son of Saul came to David, and fell on his face and did him obeisance.

"And David said, 'Mephibosheth!' And he answered, 'Behold, your servant.'

"And David said to him, 'Do not fear; for I will show you kindness for the sake of your father Jonathan, and I will restore to you all the land of Saul your father; and you shall eat at my table always' " (2 Sam. 9:6,7, *RSV*).

At one time Chile and Argentina were about to go to battle. But they came to their senses and made a pact, a covenant of peace. To commemorate that covenant, they erected a huge statue called, "The Christ of the Andes." At the bottom of that statue are these words inscribed:

"Sooner shall these mountains crumble to dust, than Chile and Argentina shall break the peace they have sworn at the feet of the Redeemer." I speak to you in the name of Christ who said, "I call you not servants, but I call you friends, for a servant does not know what his lord does" (see John 15:15).

Jesus says, "I am willing to expose My heart to you." Will you, too, expose your heart?

With one friend, or several, make a pact at the feet of the Redeemer!

1. Ask God who that friend might be.

2. Tell that friend the desires of your heart.

3. Pray about them together and plan how you will go about building a deeper friendship.

7

FIND YOUR
SPIRITUAL GIFT

You look around a church in wonder. It's an organization of volunteers; almost nobody's paid. And yet every Sunday there's a vase of beautifully arranged flowers by the pulpit. Somebody who cooks keeps turning out those church dinners. Helpful people usher, and teachers teach. . . .

The phenomenon of the gifts of the Holy Spirit exploded after the resurrection of Christ out of the grave and His glorious ascension into heaven. Do you realize that the Resurrection and the gifts of the Spirit are linked? After Christ rose, these tremendous gifts were given. This was prophesied in Psalm 68:18:

"Thou hast ascended on high, thou hast led captivity captive: thou hast received gifts for men, yea, for the rebellious also, that the Lord God might dwell among them" (*KJV*). When Paul wrote in Ephesians 4 about Christ's resurrection and the subsequent gifts of the Spirit, he quotes this very verse from the Sixty-eighth Psalm.

(Note that all God's people were to receive gifts, even the rebellious ones. Gifts are not prizes or rewards, given only to deserving Christians.)

The point is that first Christ came out of the grave and assumed His position as head of the Church. Then the Holy Spirit's power was released upon the world. And only then, a man who was a former fisherman became a tremendous evangelist—preaching with such power that after one message, three thousand confessed the Lord. And a tax collector who was formerly just a scheming little man, soon became large in his understanding, writing one of the greatest pieces of literature of all time—the Gospel of Matthew. And we could go on.

In Peter's sermon in Acts 2, he explains the sudden coming of these gifts:

"This Jesus hath God raised up, whereof we are all witnesses. Therefore, being by the right hand of God exalted, and having received from the Father the promise of the Holy Spirit, He hath shed forth this which you now see and hear." (*KJV*)

At Pentecost the risen Christ was glorified among His people. The mighty acts of God were proclaimed in the various languages of the people—a supernatural thing. Evangelism and teaching were suddenly abundant among the people. And whoosh! The church began to operate in its many-sided gifts.

Now Paul says in 1 Corinthians 12:1, ". . . concerning spiritual gifts, I do not want you to be unaware."

82

And then he goes on to show us how we are all alike, and how we are all different.

Verses 1 to 3 tell how we're alike in the Spirit. Paul says, "You know that when you were pagans . . ." (and the pagans had their vast systems of witchcraft, their trances, their dreams, their visions) *"you were led astray."* Paul says that there was a force behind the scenes, driving them to the pagan idols—a power there. Then he says,

"Therefore I make known to you, that no one speaking by the Spirit of God says, 'Jesus is accursed'; and no one can say, 'Jesus is Lord . . .'" (That's what you would call the irreducible minimum statement of Christian faith—"Jesus is Lord.") "except by the Holy Spirit" (*KJV*).

Today great exciting hosts of us around the world are saying without any hesitation, "Jesus is Lord!"

"And no man calls Jesus accursed by the Spirit of God." There is another power that says that. When some involuntary oath of cursing Christ comes out, there's an evil power behind it.

Notice that word "same"—"same Spirit"—in verses 4, 8 and 9. We have one life-power in us all. There's a lovely area north of Los Angeles called Thousand Oaks, and it does seem that there must be a thousand oaks out on the brown hillsides of that community. Each oak is different, and yet there is one oak-life that pulsates through each of those trees.

Each human body is unified because it is possessed and occupied by one person. So the body of Christ is unified because it is possessed and occupied by God Himself.

When you came to Christ, the Holy Spirit gave

you a supernatural specialty, just for you. It doesn't mean that other people may not have that—there may be many who do—but He has given you a specialty to make your Christian life fulfilled and meaningful. It isn't spooky, my friend; it's practical.

He left no one out! Verse 11:

"But one and the same Spirit works all these things, distributing to *each one individually* just as He wills." (*NASB*)

"As *He* wills." You are no more left to choose your gift, or your gifts, than you are left to choose the color of your eyes. It is just *as He wills*. I'm glad.

We are all alike in three ways: we've been influenced by the Spirit; we have been given gifts by the Spirit; and we have been baptized by the Spirit into the body of Christ.

Verse 13 says,

"For by one Spirit we were all baptized into one body, whether Jews or Greeks, whether slaves or free, and we were all made to drink of one Spirit." (*NASB*)

Now this baptism has nothing to do with water, any more than the baptism Jesus talked about when He asked, "Are you willing to be baptized with the baptism I am going to be baptized with?" These men had already been baptized with water; He was talking about the cross. Baptism does not always imply water.

The basic meaning of the word "baptism" is "to identify with." He is saying here that we are all identified by the Holy Spirit into the body of Christ—placed into the body of Christ.

This phrase "baptism of the Holy Spirit," is mentioned seven times in the New Testament. John the Baptist said, "I baptize with water; He will baptize with the Holy Spirit"—speaking of Christ. This saying is quoted in Matthew, Mark, Luke and John—that makes four times. The fifth time is Acts 1:5 where Jesus refers back to John's statement. The sixth is Acts 11:16 which refers again to what Jesus said about John's teaching. So they're very much related.

The seventh time is here in verse 13. Notice carefully that this baptism is not reserved for a select few. This verse says, "For by one Spirit we were *all* baptized. . . ." Circle the word "all." Underline it—"into one body, whether Jews or Greeks, whether slaves or free. . . ." It doesn't have anything to do with our situation in life, whether we are super-spiritual or not. *We were all made to drink of one Spirit.*

Two plus two equals four in everything but theology! Somehow, when you get to theology it's a free-for-all! Some Christians say, "I don't know what theology says, but I believe so-and-so." Listen, theology is a study of God! Theology is the study of the Word of God! It's the queen of the sciences. We want to be very careful to keep words clear and to use them only as God uses them.

First Corinthians 12:13 says that all Christians are baptized into the body of Christ by the Holy Spirit—that this is common to all Christians. The baptism of the Spirit is not anything to divide us into the "have's" and the "have not's," rather all "have"! We are all united, according to God's Word, by our common baptism into the body of Christ.

Maybe some of the Corinthians were using the term "baptism of the Holy Spirit" as a "second work of grace" subsequent to conversion, and Paul is correcting this here. Look at the verbs in this verse: "For by one Spirit we *were* all baptized"—it's an aorist, or past tense—"we *were* baptized into the body of Christ." When? When Jesus gloriously forgave your sins and placed you into His family. When you became His child, He identified you. He thrust you into the body of Christ. If you want to use the meaning of the word as "immersed"—He immersed you forever into Christ. "For by one Spirit we were all baptized into one body." We *were*. It happened when we believed, whether we are Jews or Greeks, slaves or free, we *were* all made—past tense—as part of His body to drink of that Spirit.

Baptism into the Body is one happening, but the filling of the Holy Spirit—ah, my friend, the apostles were filled, and then they were filled, and then they were filled again—the same people—many times! That must be a continuous, flowing of the Spirit of God upon your life. That must be maintained with great care and openness to God and to His work in you. Let us be Spirit-filled Christians! Paul says, "Be ye 'being filled' with the Spirit"—that's what it means. Keep on being filled with the Spirit.

The New Testament gives one huge cry for unity. Oh, it calls out for oneness! Jesus continually says, "As the branches are one in the vine, as the sheep are one in the fold, as the building blocks are one in the building, be one in Me." It's a terrible thing to Jesus for the Body to be separated or divided.

Now, "point two" is that we are all different. Verses 4,5:

"There are varieties of gifts, but the same Spirit.

And there are varieties of ministries, and the same Lord." (*NASB*)

The human body is the illustration: it has many "members," or parts, and they're all different. Your ear is different from your hair; and your eye is different from your arm. This is what makes the body useful, and God says, "That's what I want you to be, together, as My people. Just like that!"

There are four lists of the various gifts in the New Testament, and Paul gives them all—Romans chapter 12; 1 Corinthians 12, in this first part of the chapter; again in verses 28 to 30 in the second part of the chapter; and then another list in Ephesians 4. Twenty-nine different gifts are listed in all.

The gift of prophecy is in each of the various lists. (By the way, if you want to know what prophecy is, it's in 1 Corinthians 14:3, "The one who prophesies speaks to men for edification and exhortation and consolation." It's just speaking out God's truth.) And God gives teachers, and evangelists, and pastors, and the ministry of helping others. I said to a man in my study the other day, "It's obvious to us all that God has given you the gift of helping others. We ask you to do something, and you do it 'yesterday.' And you seem to do it so easily and so joyously."

Remember these gifts are supernatural. They are not just common talents. God may take a natural talent and endow it with the Holy Spirit at conversion so that the convert moves into a new orbit with that ministry. Or He may not at all. He may "start from scratch," and as the new believer is baptized by the Spirit into the body of Christ, he is given a new gift—or several.

I don't think the lists from these four sections of Scripture are meant to be all inclusive. In our present space age, for example, God can add other gifts and just expand the church. Maybe some are not as important as others. But the same Spirit of God flows and works and moves and empowers the church, and makes the church glorify Christ and enables the members to help one another.

The thing I want us to see is this: no Christian should ever say, "I have no gift." That simply is not true. You can find your gift by seeing those things you do which are helpful to the rest of the believers, which you do with ease by the Spirit of God. Frankly, I don't know any place in the Scripture that tells us how to find what our gifts are. I suspect the Lord doesn't want us to get hung up on introspection and start taking aptitude tests. Evidently the Spirit who gives the gifts is the One who can easily tell you what yours are, and maybe tell your brother's, too, in case you need counsel about it.

But look at the list of the gifts and ask, "Lord, where do I serve in the Body!" And be glad for your gifts! Be glad for other people's gifts; rejoice in them. Fit yourself together with the Body of Christ.

Listen, for you not to use your gift is a terrible thing. It's like severing a portion of the body to withhold yourself in this way. If a hand is suddenly severed, it's repulsive! But when my hand is upon my arm, and I reach it out to you and say, "Brother, good morning," you say, "That's warm and good. I like that."

The last verse says, "Earnestly desire the greater gifts." I can't believe it means that all of us should get whatever we want. This passage already said the gifts are given to us as the Spirit wills. But rather, as a Body of believers—it's a plural thought—we should desire the gifts among our particular group that are the best gifts for us; those that are going to help us to minister to our area and around the world in great power. God isn't making "big shots," my friend; He isn't interested in that. He's interested in making people fit into the family of God and make the work of the gospel "go."

And He says the way is love. "I show you a more excellent way."

Listen, whatever you know as a Christian, you don't know much yet if you haven't learned the exhilaration of "putting it together" in the Spirit with other believers, of humbling yourself to say, "I'm one with you, my brother." And of being bold enough and full of faith enough to say, "Look, here's what I am. Here's what I can contribute. I'll submit to whatever way the rest of you in the Body want to use me!"

1. List abilities you have that God could use to support and encourage others—music, cooking, construction work, being friendly—anything. Circle abilities you want God to begin using.

2. Talk to God about fears, insecurities and other problems which prevent His using all your abilities in any way He wants.

3. Ask God about any gifts He would especially like to develop in you. Talk to Him about your availability, barriers and what He wants you to do.

8

YOUNG, FEMININE AND CHRISTIAN

Have you realized that when the apostle Paul crossed over from Acts chapter 15 to Acts 16, that was some crossing? For the first time in his life he crossed from Asia to Europe. He crossed from a strictly man's world to a setup like most of our English-speaking world today.

Maybe his mouth dropped open that first Sabbath in Philippi when he went to a prayer meeting of women!

And, of all things, a *woman* asked him to stay in her home—a woman in business for herself, selling expensive purple fabric. Jerusalem was never like this!

For several years Paul preached and lived in the European world, finally settling in Corinth where he lived, not at a man's house but at a couple's house. Aquila and Priscilla were more than just married;

they both worked at tent-making; they both helped straighten out Apollos' doctrine; they both traveled with Paul in the ministry. He loved them both! But all this was some switch from Asia!

And interesting, when Paul later writes back to the European churches where women were prominent in the scene, we discover what we know anyway: that women not only add graces to a situation but complicate it, too. Paul has problems to speak to when he writes the Corinthians or Philippians, for instance, that couldn't possibly come up among the Galatians or Ephesians.

Let's see what the church letters have to say about you women—and about-to-be women.

Chapters 5 and 6 of 1 Corinthians deal with sex, good and bad, mostly among married people. But chapter 6 ends with a solid word of conclusion for everybody, including high-school-age gals:

". . . Run from sex sin! No other sin affects the body as this one does. When you sin this sin, it is against your own body" (1 Cor. 6:18, *TLB*).

In other words, do yourself a favor: don't hurt *yourself* by getting involved sexually! You will get hurt, get scarred. God wants you to save these wonderful pleasures for marriage later. The reason?

"Haven't you yet learned that your body is the home of the Holy Spirit . . . ?" (v. 19).

Fantastic! If you're a Christian your very body is God's home. Oh, treat it well, with all the dignity, beauty, modesty and grace you can! Let your looks and bodily actions be a great advertisement that God's Holy Spirit lives inside. Did you catch His name? Holy.

Now let's begin with chapter 7, verse 25:

"What about girls who are not yet married? Should they be permitted to do so?"

"*Permitted*—?" you're saying. "Well, you just better believe it!" But, actually, Paul goes on in verses 26-28 to explain that the world then was in tough times—as it is today—and that for work of God, Christians must think soberly about whether they can best serve Him as single or married.

I know single Christians doing Bible translation work in places families could never go. And when five missionary men were martyred by Auca Indians in Ecuador, who went into the tribe to give them the gospel—and got away with it? A young widow, her baby and a single woman! Those who are seemingly helpless in this world can move into tough spots for God where the strong can't go!

Single girls, ask God if He wants to put you in one of those fabulously strategic places. You couldn't have a more rewarding life. The world would say you're cheated. Well, don't be pushed into the mold of this world's thinking patterns, but "be transformed by the renewing of your minds" (Rom. 12:2). Then you'll have 20-20 vision to see from God's perspective what His perfect will is for you.

Paul's not against marriage! This same Paul wrote the gorgeous togetherness of Ephesians 5. His only point is this: if your ambition is to get married—that's worldly. If your ambition is to do God's will and it can be better done with a husband, God will provide.

Just don't be over-occupied about it! Hang loose! (See 1 Cor. 7:32.)

Now turn to 1 Corinthians 11, where you see God's hierarchy: first God, then Christ, then the man, then the woman (v. 3). Now, before you think you're low "woman" on the totem pole—this hierarchy has nothing to do with superiority and inferiority. Christ is not less than God the Father. He is equal to Him, being, in fact, also God! But in His *role* as the Son (and that word "role" is the key) He subjected Himself to the Father's will—even "learning obedience through the things He suffered."

So a godly man learns submission (through pressures, through suffering) to the will of Christ and God. And a godly woman learns submission (it ain't easy!) to the will of her godly man. Again, she's not *inferior* to nor less than man. (No women are more exalted and cared for than those in Christian cultures.) But her role is to be in submission to the man. When she tries to be above him she interferes with the workable hierarchy.

So, says 1 Corinthians 11:5, the application of this is for a woman to have her head covered in church.

Don't panic, girls! All the Bible is God's Word, and every bit of it is there for a reason, but occasionally something from first-century culture pops up. (Like the classic "greet one another with a holy kiss.") Then we have to ask, "What is the underlying principle here to be translated into our culture?"

Well, do you come striding aggressively into your high school Sunday School department like you're ten feet tall? Or—and this is a subtle thing, but you gals are wonderfully subtle creatures—do you come in with the psychological feeling that something's on your head? Do you come to Sunday School knowing everything and having all the answers?

Come with an attitude that you're here to learn something from the Lord and from your brothers and sisters in the class. Come in a spirit of modesty, quietness, femininity, teachability, deferring to your Christian brothers and sisters. Don't try to outdo them in appearing spiritual! Admire and encourage whatever level of godliness they've acquired. Followers can turn into leaders if you back off and give them a chance. That doesn't mean you don't participate. You have good ideas too! But share your ideas in the spirit of a learner, not in the spirit of a know-it-all.

Ephesians 6 talks about your role as a daughter. Verse 1 deals with the years you're under your parents' roof, subject to their directions. Verse 2 deals with your relationship with them forever. In verse 1 you obey. In verse 2 you honor.

Do you feel as a teen-ager you're somewhere in between? It's hard, isn't it—being half in and half out of the nest! Jesus was twelve when He first expressed His growing transference of obedience away from His earthly father and to His heavenly Father (Luke 2:49). But your folks are still paying the bills and are legally responsible for you. So "learn obedience by the things that you suffer"—especially if your parents are not Christians—and establish a relationship that will keep you honoring them, considering their opinions and so on.

First Peter 3:1-6 is a wonderful description of a spiritual woman. If this kind will make an ungodly husband turn around, it must be good for any of you.

This woman's beauty may or may not be on the outside, but God looks on the inside for that "meek and quiet spirit" (v. 3). Are you cringing, saying, "I'm anything but meek and quiet?" Praise God for Matthew 9:20-22, the story of the hemorrhaging woman! Jesus healed her *from the inside out*. Bystanders probably didn't realize a difference, except for the glow on her face. So He can heal your agitated spirit.

This "lasting" or "incorruptible" charm goes on 'til you're 99! And remember, meekness is not weakness. Actually, it's harder than the other. Meekness is strength under control.

"Precious to God" means that this spirit is a rare commodity. And as we survey women in general, we have to say, "That's right. This kind of woman is in the minority—but of great value to God."

Does the biblical view of a woman seem hampering? Well, remember that a bird is only free as long as he's in the air, in the sphere where God wants him to be. A fish is only free in water, God's place for him.

In these all-important, molding, shaping years, practice staying in God's sphere for you. Practice it at home, at church, in all your relationships. It will prepare you to be a beautiful woman of God some day—mature, fulfilled, and free!

Think what it would mean for you, or gals you know, to be young women of the Lord:

1. What would a girl be like who treats her body with dignity? beauty? modesty? grace? How would she act? dress? talk? etc.

2. If a Christian's body is God's home, describe

the girl who is a "good advertisement" of God's presence within.

3. Write out what it means to be submissive; to clothe oneself in modesty; to have a quiet, gentle spirit; for a girl to "sense her femininity." Check your ideas with several friends, your mom and with some older women in your church.

4. Girls, on a 3x5-inch card write, "You are a daughter of God and the Holy Spirit dwells in you! Yahoo!" Post it where you will see it every morning. Praise God for your womanhood when you read it.

9

YOUNG, MANLY AND CHRISTIAN

When I was a teen-ager I knew God was calling me into the ministry. In fact, I can't remember when He wasn't. I guess what really bothered me most was that my image of a pastor was a less-than-rugged, colorless person who didn't have any fun!

I suppose that my view of a minister was pretty much the same as my view of a godly guy.

Right under my nose, within my own home, were my two big brothers, who were a living contradiction of all my fears. They were rugged, fun, and godly! It was these guys who kept the option open for me to be young, manly and Christian. I thank God for them!

How do you become a godly young man? How do you get life all together?

This kind of guy cannot swing along with every current fad. The youth scene changes like a pendulum; it swings from one extreme to another. The world goes from one "kick" to an opposite emphasis. The Christian too often changes along with the world around him.

The Bible, not the current "in thing," gives young men specific guidelines for becoming mature.

Here's the plan: (1) the young man himself; (2) the young man of God in the home; (3) in the church; and (4) in his ministry.

When God begins something very special He often starts with a young man. Daniel is an example. He was young (Dan. 1:4); he was committed. "Daniel made up his mind that he would not defile himself with the king's choice food . . ." (Dan. 1:8, *NASB*). He had high standards. Culture and society were not going to determine his life-style. God alone was to do that. But he graciously and tactfully asked for permission to eat in a way that God would approve. (See Dan. 1:11,12.) The result? God honored Daniel and his friends, and blessed him with wisdom. Daniel became a world leader.

Jeremiah is another example of God choosing a young man to do a great work.

"Now the word of the Lord came to me saying, 'Before I formed you in the womb I knew you. And before you were born I consecrated you; I have appointed you a prophet to the nations.'

"Then I said, 'Alas, Lord God! Behold I do not know how to speak, because I am a youth.'

"But the Lord said to me, 'Do not say, "I am a youth," because everywhere I send you, you shall go, and all that I command you, you shall speak. Do not be afraid of them, For I am with you to deliver you,' declares the Lord" (Jer. 1:4-8, *NASB*).

Jeremiah himself records this to show us how God prepared him and appointed him to be a young force for Himself.

Great historic revivals have come from God through young men. John and Charles Wesley were young brothers whom God used to "tell it like it is." George Whitfield, also part of the Great Awakening in England and America, was a young man who reached the masses for Christ. So it was with Charles Spurgeon, and many others.

Earlier we mentioned the students at Williams College in Massachusetts, who were out praying for the world. It began to rain and the fellows found shelter under the overhang of the haystack. There they got a vision for missions. Out of that "Haystack Prayer Meeting" of young men came the world's modern missionary movement.

We could go on and on. But don't get a "big head"! God also uses old people. Pride can keep you from God's best. One young man who thought he knew everything finally surrendered to God's will and said, "I have resigned as the general manager of the universe!"

Guys, Christ is Lord—your Lord. Your body is His. Your mind is Christ's. Your emotions are for Him. Christ is Lord. Now, how does this become practical?

Ephesians 6:1-4 is a key passage here. The Apostle introduced this section on the home with a general direction to all, in 5:21: "Be subject to one another, in the fear of Christ." One of the chief things you must learn to do is to surrender, adapt yourself, fit in with one another.

99

One night my daughter sat out in a car after a date for a half hour or so. (It seemed like six hours to me!) When she came in I said, "Hey, no more of that sitting out in the car like that with a guy. Come on into the house if you've got more to say." She said with a shocked, innocent look, "Why, Dad, don't you trust me?" I looked her in the eye and replied, "No, I don't! I don't trust myself; why should I trust you?" Only Christ can be absolutely relied on.

None of us is trustworthy. Jesus said our hearts are full of sin. We desperately need loving restraint from those who are concerned about us.

You can help make your parents great. When Abraham brought his son Isaac up Mount Moriah, that must have been a tense time! But Isaac was quietly obedient, even though he didn't know what was going to happen. Because of Isaac's attitude, Abraham could pull off that whole experience. He did not "bug" his dad for answers about what was coming, nor resist him. He and Abraham must have had a beautiful relationship. Isaac said, "I see the rope, wood and so forth, but where is the animal for offering?" Abraham answered, "God will provide Himself a lamb, Son!" That's heavy faith! Isaac helped his dad become great—by quiet support.

Guys, if you only knew how hard it is to be a dad! Some day you will know how inadequate a dad can feel. My kids have helped me to become what I never could have been without them—because they have supported me in spite of my inadequacies.

Our ten-year-old guy talks to everyone he sees. And before the conversation gets very far he's told our family history. In the midst of it somewhere he will say, "I've got neat parents." I feel supported—unworthy, true—but supported.

The godly guy treats his brothers and sisters with respect. Remember Ephesians 5:21 applies here. "Fit in"—or adapt yourself—to them, too. Our permissive culture may say that fighting and arguing are normal and inevitable, but that's not God's way. Godly guys are not sarcastic to brothers and sisters. If you tend to be this way, get to God; confess it; and start to love and respect them.

But listen! Get hold of this great truth: your natural family is actually only temporary. You are responsible there. But you have in Christ a supernatural family that is eternal. They're going to be your family forever! And they take shape now in the local church. Give them a high priority in your life!

The apostle Paul gave young Timothy instruction on how to live with the spiritual family in 1 Timothy 5:1-3. What about the older men in your church? Consider them very precious and important. "Do not sharply rebuke an older man, but rather appeal to him as a father." Too many times Christian young men counsel with no one. Yet God says they are to appeal to the wisdom and experience of older men in Christ.

First Kings 12:6-11 gives the tragic story of a young king who took only the counsel of young friends and rejected the counsel of older men. It ended in bad news!

Years ago I made a request that when the time came my son would call in a group of "fathers in Christ" to counsel him about his career, men who had watched him grow up and who knew his gifts and abilities. This he did. What assurance God gave him as he started out on his life's work.

And then the guys your own age: Treat them as brothers. They are your family in the deepest, most eternal sense, not competition you try to beat out! Enjoy each other.

Treat older women as mothers. What keen insights they often have. They are so comfortable to be with. Don't be shy; love them, ask their advice; bridge the gap.

Treat young women as "sisters, in all purity." Whether on a date or at school, give them your highest and best—your purest. They are more emotional and can be easily hurt. They are not often as logical as men. But they are often right—amazing intuition these women have!

You'll probably be friends with many, date some, and go bananas over one! But treat them all as sisters in Christ, "in all purity."

How is the godly young man to minister? Paul tells Titus what to teach young men:

"Likewise urge the young men to be sensible; in all things show yourself to be an example of good deeds, with purity in doctrine, dignified, sound in speech which is beyond reproach, in order that the opponent may be put to shame, having nothing bad to say about us" (Titus 2:6-8, *NASB*).

Here is a strong appeal to be self-controlled. Live sensibly; don't go off on doctrinal tangents and do strange things. We are all a little nutty! You have it in you to be an "odd ball." Be sensible—get advice from God and key men of God. Ask God to make you live a dignified life-style. Remember, you are "something else!" You have Christ inside!

Unless you are stable, the world around you will judge the Christian life as something for strange people only. By your steadiness, "opponents" will be put to shame (v. 8). They will not be able to deny the superiority of living with Christ.

John the Apostle wrote about young men in 1 John 2:13,14:

"I am writing to you, young men, because you have overcome the evil one. I have written to you, children, because you know the father. . . . I have written to you, young men, because you are strong, and the word of God abides in you, and you have overcome the evil one" (*NASB*).

You will need to resist the "evil one." He'll give you plenty of practice at this! You do it by knowing the Word. You must be like Christ, who resisted temptation by saying, "It is written." The Word will make you strong. Memorize it! Love it! Use it! Let it "abide" in you.

This will mean making a daily schedule—to put your life together so that you give top time to the Word and prayer.

Young brother, be a man of God. This will mean you must be a man of vision. Joel says that in the last days, "Young men will see visions" (Joel 2:25; Acts 2:17). Have days alone with God for prayer to get vision. Let God adjust your eyes for the future of your life, "Go for broke" with Him!

What it comes down to, is surrendering to Christ as Lord. Men, we are in an authority crisis. A new book out by Howard Butt has a great title: *The Velvet*

Covered Brick. The brick stands for strict authority. The velvet is the tenderness that surrounds and clothes it. Christ was a humble servant (velvet) but authority as Lord (brick). My friend, until you're willing to be a servant, you can in no way be a leader. It's not hard to accept submission from one who himself has submitted! Unsubmissive authority is repressive and revolting. Top people who are broken, we can follow with dignity.

Jesus is that! He submitted to the cross, was broken for us—but He arose with total authority.

You can be that in Christ.

Young man, be a velvet covered brick.

Let's begin thinking through what that means for you and teen-age young men you know:

1. Get a pencil and paper. Then review this chapter and list qualities which are traits of a "man of God." Fellows, talk to God about the list and the areas where you need to grow.

2. What are the different barriers which make it hard for young men to submit to God's authority? Are any of these barriers preventing you or young men you know from completely making Christ Lord?

3. What notable characteristics distinguish a young man who "has it together" from a Christian young man who is living as a "man of God"? Young men, how will you make these notable parts of your life?

4. Fellows, ask your dad (if he's a Christian), or some other older man in your church, to be a "father in Christ" to you and help you mature as God's man. Let him read this chapter too. Then talk and pray together about how you can grow in this new relationship.

10

"AROUND THE HOUSE"

There were two porcupines living in Alaska. It was very cold. To keep warm, they decided to draw close together. But when they did that, they needled each other. So they pulled apart. But again they got cold. And so they moved close again and they got needled. It was very frustrating because these porcupines were continuously cold or else needling one another.

That's the way some people live in their homes. At a distance they are lonely and cold. But when they draw near they needle and hurt one another.

I don't believe we need to live that way. I believe that God wants us to be able to draw close and be very warm and comfortable together.

But there are obstacles to this unity that I'm talking about. Just let me reconstruct for you what happens in the average home.

When a guy (or a gal) gets married, there is just

one person he really has to satisfy. And even that isn't always easy!

Maybe he's noisy, eats huge meals, ransacks the refrigerator all the time. And he's a very easygoing fellow. Where he grew up everyone came and went when they wished and ate what they wanted. But his new wife comes from a very quiet, orderly home. Everybody was restrained.

Pretty soon he's singing,

> "Why don't we get along?
> Everything I do is wrong;
> Tell me, what's the reason
> I'm not pleasin' you?"

Well, as poet Edgar A. Guest said, "It takes a heap o' living to make a house a home." And it takes plain hard work to build unity there.

Speaking of marriages, G. K. Chesterton, that wise Roman Catholic philosopher, said, "I have known many marriages, but never a compatible one." What he meant was this, that when people come together under one roof there's already a built-in, ready-made incompatibility. The two married people come from different backgrounds and different ways of doing things. And the kids have more and more outside influences adding to and reshaping their thinking. It takes plenty of work to keep continually adjusting to each other.

When a family first begins, the new married couple has only one interpersonal relationship. That's enough to work on. But then the first child comes. There are *three* interpersonal relationships that can go awry: mother and dad, baby and mother, and baby and dad.

Think what happens when two children come into that home. There are six interpersonal relationships that have to be kept clear. But that's nothing; when four children are in that home there are fifteen interpersonal relationships that can get out of focus. If there are five children, there are twenty-one interpersonal relationships that can go awry. With six, there are twenty-eight!

Now, how many must you adjust to in *your* home? How many people must adjust to you? Think about it. Each relationship is important—potentially devastating!

Recently I left home for three weeks, and I took away four interpersonal relationships from our home. When I flew away on the plane, so did trouble! Interpersonal relationships in our household went down from ten to six. Things got a lot simpler!

Think what happens when grandparents come to visit a family, say, of six. Suddenly they have twenty-eight interpersonal relationships! The children say, "Hey, what's going on around here?" But think of it the other way. When a family of six comes into a quiet little home of grandmother and grandfather, suddenly, instead of one, there are twenty-eight interpersonal relationships in that home. They love their family, but when they all go the grandparents say, "Phew-w-w." And Granddad says to Grandmother, "I guess I'm getting old." No, Granddad, you just had twenty-seven interpersonal relationships walk in on you. That's a whirlwind!

Now transfer all this to your home. It's an arena of action. Suppose Mother gets sick with all the family depending on one another. The ironing stacks up, the meals get poor, and the children begin to "climb the wall."

Home is a place where one has to work on these interpersonal relationships. Home is where there ought to be peace, because you count it as the most important place in all the world.

In an old *Life* magazine I read,

"The businessman gives service with a smile: he is deferential to his boss, his customers and usually even to his underlings. Women are polite to their neighbors and to door-to-door salesmen. Hardly a voice is raised in anger except behind the closed doors of the home. As the outside world becomes more and more constrained, more and more people seem to feel that the home is the last remaining place where they can quit kidding and be their own ornery selves.

"The bride and groom who have been standing so patiently in the reception line, smiling sweetly at people they hardly know, or the young people putting on the act at school and church can seem ornery indeed to each other when they get home and let down their hair."

Isn't that true? Haven't you caught yourself being mean at home, and great to almost everybody else? There are plenty of obstacles—but we need to change the spirit of our homes to loving unity.

How can you change the spirit of the home where you live? There are progressive steps.

FIRSTLY, realize you already have something going for you in the very makeup of the home. *God created the family.* First He made a man. Then He said, "It is not good for man to live alone." The first thing about creation that God said was "not good" was man's aloneness. So He gave man a wife. He began human life with a family.

Then, remember, the world became very sinful on earth. So God sent the flood, and gave this world a new start with Noah and his family. *God began again with a family.*

Then God chose a nation, Israel, as we read in Genesis, chapter 12. And when He did, He began with a family. God loves families. He just loves the home! Indeed, the family is the basic unit in God's economy.

There's a oneness in the family. You live in the same place. There's oneness by your name, and your food. You have a oneness because of your memories that are built together. From the very beginning, little Junior begins to walk like his daddy, and the children begin to talk like their parents. Mother and Dad even begin to look alike after awhile.

SECONDLY, we get unity in our home life by a definite step of faith. We must believe in the Lord Jesus Christ. When we're saved, God begins right there, and gives us a deeper unity. He places us into the body of Christ, so that the members of the family, having trusted in the Lord Jesus, have a new relationship in depth. They are in the family of God, brothers and sisters in Christ. They have the same Holy Spirit. They have the same Lord. The Christian home has a lot going for it! It is a wonderful, new thing God does when we believe. The Christian home is the Christian church in miniature!

Let's look now at the Scriptures. In Ephesians 4:1-3, we are told what the relationship is within the family of God. Paul, in chapter 4, talks about the family of the mother and father and the children. He says, "I therefore, a prisoner for the Lord, beg you to lead a life worthy of the calling to which you have been called" (*RSV*).

He says you are to lead a life "with all lowliness and meekness, with patience, forbearing one another in love, eager to maintain the unity of the Spirit in the bond of peace." Notice that word "maintain." We are related to the same Christ. We should cherish and nourish this unity. We should love it and live as though we are really in this unity. Mother and Father, your children are also your brothers and sisters in Christ. And young people, your Christian parents are your brother and sister in Christ.

The Christian home has an intensified relationship as the little church—the mother and father who love Jesus, and boys and girls who honor the Saviour—come together to live.

This is the idea we have in Ephesians 5, verses 28 and following: "Even so, husbands should love their wives as their own bodies." Speaking of unity—this is really amazing, isn't it? "He who loves his wife loves himself. For no man ever hates his own flesh, but nourishes and cherishes it, as Christ does the church, because we are members of his body. For this reason a man shall leave his father and mother and be joined to his wife, and the two shall become one'" (*RSV*).

I notice that Paul goes on to say, "This is a great mystery." And when I've read this, I've said, "I don't understand it." A man should love his wife as he loves himself. Because he loves his wife, Paul says, he is loving himself. The Holy Spirit is speaking to us here of the depth of the relationship of a man and a woman—how much a part of each other they become. They become one.

THIRDLY, build unity in your home not only by appropriating this gift of God by faith, but also by exercising *obedience.* I believe that obedience means that a man takes his place as head of the house; and the woman takes her place as the wife and mother of the home; and the children remain children, obedient and loving. In other words, we take our God-assigned roles in the family relationship.

"The husband," says Ephesians 5:23, "is the head of the wife, as Christ is the head of the church, his body, and is himself its Savior" (*RSV*).

Verse 25 says, "Husbands, love your wives as Christ loved the church and gave himself up for her."

God calls us men to be Christlike in our attitudes, Christlike in our leadership in our homes. Christ died for us. Christ lives for us—the church. At times the husband is to reject his own comforts and interests because the ones he loves the most deserve his attention. He is willing to give himself to his family. That's what Christ did for the human race.

It's true, young people, that given a few years of school, maybe even college, you get pretty bright—maybe in some subjects smarter than your parents. The point is not who is smarter. The point is the hierarchy that God has ordained: who in the family He's appointed to be president of the corporation, who vice-president, and so on.

But leadership must be given. Don't make your parents continually struggle for it!

An interviewer was talking to a couple on a television show recently. He asked the woman, "And who is the head of your house?" She said, "My husband is." He thought he would be clever, so he said, "Who decided that?" She said, "I did."

Ho, ho, ho! That was to be a cue for a big guffaw. But actually, you see, she's absolutely right. No one else could decide it. You see, the husband is not to take leadership, the wife is to *give* it—allow it. She is to submit to her place, just as he is to assume his place. The parents can no longer demand leadership—from a son who's taller than they are. He's to give it because he understands his God-given role.

And of course, there has to be a mutual finding of one another. Mothers and dads, children, brothers and sisters have to talk about their roles. Talk about what you want from each other, the kind of son or daughter you want to be, what you expect of them. You've got to talk it out, and find the biblical ways to build unity.

"Children," says Ephesians 6:1,2, "obey your parents in the Lord, for this is right. 'Honor your father and mother' (this is the first commandment with a promise)." A child must learn to obey. He is to obey until he leaves the home. Of course, as the children get older, wise parents begin to loosen the reins some and let the children assume more responsibilities. But essentially, the wise parent expects his child to obey and the wise young person expects to obey until he leaves father and cleaves unto his wife. And then he is to establish his own family with the same standards he has learned while a child in his own home.

Ephesians 6:2 says that children are to honor their

parents. I don't think there's any age limit on that. As long as God lets you have your mother and father, honor them! After they're gone, honor their memory. A home should have a picture of Grandmother and Grandfather. Let your growing children look into the eyes of their grandparents to remember their faith and to remember their heritage.

Incidentally, if you're a Christian young person in a non-Christian home, or with one parent not a Christian, your behavior is the very thing that will bring Christ to your loved ones! Being an obedient young person to an unbelieving parent isn't always easy, but these are the very areas of your life where the Holy Spirit's power can show itself.

Young people, today you are a different new generation of young people. I believe that young people among us have a different challenge than we've had. Somehow, the world seems to have been thrown at you, all at once. I was reading this in *Christian Education Trends*:

"Why do teens and college students feel entitled to hold an opinion on everything, indict their parents, sit in judgment over authorities? Television viewing may be a significant part of the answer. This present generation of college students is the first with lifelong exposure to TV.

"Speaking in Toronto on 'Children and Television' one authority likened the American situation to that of children in a primitive tribe on a Pacific island. For children there experience everything that everyone is doing in the tribe. The children are everywhere. There are no secrets. There is no privacy."[3]

And in a sense, that is the experience of many

young people of today. Through the TV screen you've been exposed to the marriage problems, violence, intimate bedroom scenes and to the whole world. You do know a great deal intellectually, but emotionally, it's very difficult for you. I think you need compassion more than any other generation of young people.

I'd like to say this to you young people: Remember, because you may have *information* does not mean you have *wisdom*. There is something of wisdom that only years can give. Learn to sit down and look into the eyes of gray-haired people, and find out what life is all about.

There are many problems in the home today, and there are many wonderful opportunities. How are you going to make all this work out? Frankly, I think there's only one way. Ephesians 5:21 says to husbands, wives and children "Be subject to one another out of reverence for Christ" (*RSV*). We have to adjust ourselves in the home to the proper role of our proper place of responsibility.

Remember, Jesus said not to go into your relationships judging others. "Judge not" (Matt. 7:1). He says that a judgmental attitude is really like a person having a plank in his eye and saying to someone who has a little speck in his eye, "Let me help you take that speck out of your eye." You know what the person with the little speck is going to say? "No thanks."

Jesus says, come into your family relationships with deep humility. In Galatians 5:13-16 we have a good word on this:

"For you were called to freedom, brethren; only do not use your freedom as an opportunity for the flesh, but through love be servants of one another. For the whole law is fulfilled in one word, 'You shall love your neighbor as yourself.' But if you bite and devour one another take heed that you are not consumed by one another" (*RSV*).

Call a moratorium on all biting and devouring in your home! Say, "No more of that business. In our home we're going to respect and love each other. We are *not* going to be critical." And then go to God with your own sins. "For if we confess our sins, he is faithful and just to forgive us our sins and to cleanse us from all unrighteousness" (1 John 1:9, *RSV*).

My friend, bend low and go to the cross. Confession is not only vertical toward God, but it is horizontal toward those whom you offend. If you've been like a porcupine at home, go to those you've offended, and tell them that! And God will bring peace and unity to your home.

Work on yourselves, by the Spirit of God. Let Him make you into that obedient, humble, kindly, young person you want to be. How do you do it? Just by coming to the cross and admitting that in yourself you cannot do this, then drawing your strength from Christ.

We've seen too many supposedly happy and wonderful homes shaken right to the foundation. We know that it takes the grace of God to have a happy home. God bless you as you come together to the cross and there let Christ work unity into your home. This will truly give you a taste of heaven here on earth!

Let's take a look at you in your family:

1. How many possible interpersonal relationships

are there in your family? How many of these do you directly affect?

2. Set your mind to be positive about those in your family. On a piece of paper make a chart. Down the left side list all the traits named in Philippians 4:8 of good thinking—true, honorable, lovely, etc.

Across the page make a column for each person in your family. In the columns list traits of each person which are good to think about according to the list on the left. Then think on these things!

If you have trouble thinking of good things to say, start your list by writing, "God gave him/her to me as a special gift to love."

3. Set aside a time this week when you will pray for the members of your family. Remember both to express thankfulness and make requests.

4. List the names of each person in your family and one way you will express peace and love toward each person this week.

5. Are there any areas in which you find it especially difficult to be obedient, honor your parents, or be noncritical? If so, talk to the Lord about those areas and ask Him to help change your attitude.

COMMITMENT 3

Commit yourself to
the world—your work
in it, your witness
to it.

Back and forth wash the in-and-out tides over the years: separate yourself from the world and be holy . . . get in there and witness . . . be different . . . be salt . . . be distinct . . . be involved . . . be out of the world . . . be in the world. . . .

"Out" periods, no doubt, foster lack of dialogue with the world, but they bring a great sense of truly being the people of God.

"In" periods—like now—give us closeness to the worldlings and a sympathy for them, but often not enough holiness and biblical knowledge to help them out of the world.

"Out" periods breed legalism. "In" periods breed license.

What's the proper balance?

Back to our wheel.

First we construct the hub. *I center my life on attending to God.* I will give Him the firstfruits of my time each day, sitting before Him. I will adore Him, study Him, and obey Him. I will learn the discipline of living continually in His presence.

Next, by following Commitment Two, I fit the spokes carefully into place. I will consciously put the Body ahead of work. I will love and serve my brothers and sisters. I will minister to them through my spiritual gifts; I will strengthen them in God. I will relate to one or several closest to me on the deepest level—expecting them to discipline me in my weaknesses, and in turn, expecting to exhort, rebuke, and guide them from my strengths.

When the hub and spokes are fitted together, the rim—the third commitment—takes its position and its right amount of importance.

Let's define the rim. It's my place in this world—economically, politically, spiritually, in every way. It's my work contribution to it. I clean house, cut the lawn, fix cars, babysit, volunteer at the hospital, keep up with my homework, serve as a class officer, pick up some groceries at the store for my folks, fix a toy for a younger brother. It's what my physical body adds to make the world happen.

It's my intellectual contribution to it. I share ideas in class, talk things over with my friends at lunch, discuss things with my parents, write for the school paper. I contribute a thought, and someone sees things in a new way.

It's my spiritual contribution. Out of the flow of Commitments One and Two comes, "I've got to tell you what I found in Colossians 2 this afternoon" . . .

"Hal, I love you too much not to say it: you'll never find yourself without Jesus Christ" . . . plus a thousand thousand "Praise Gods" and "Alleluias."

At Lake Avenue we'd spent a couple of years getting our feet wet in the Company of the Committed. With much failure and a little success, we'd been asking God to help us as a people to put Him first and to place each other second.

It was New Year's Eve, the beginning of the church's diamond anniversary year. We were enjoying God together as a church family; it was about 10:30 P.M.

I said, "What can we ask God for in our seventy-fifth year?"

The Minister of Visitation got to his feet. Bless him! What a team member. "Well," he said, "The number 7-5-0 keeps coming into my mind. Why don't we keep track as a congregation of all those we win to Christ this year and ask the Lord for seven hundred fifty?"

Everyone broke into applause! It seemed breathtaking, but wonderful.

At the end of the next December, the stack of cards from our individual witnessing reported that 930 new converts had been born into the family of God.

11

COPE WITH TODAY'S WORLD

One Saturday morning about 7:30 some of us men were gathered for prayer. Suddenly that place began to shake with a California earthquake that really rattled our back teeth!

There's a rumble in all of society today. It's everywhere; you can't escape it. I'd like us to try to understand the problem and see how we Christians must have some special insight for solving it.

There is a new mood among us, a new restlessness all over the world. I don't think it's just a few young radicals flexing their muscles. We miss it altogether unless we understand that a national—in fact, a worldwide—mood of disenchantment has really hit us. Of course, there are a few hard-core, violent radicals, but there is also a ground swell of unrest among almost all people.

If we take a backward look maybe we can better understand the young and the old. In 1925 Calvin Coolidge said, "The business of America is business." Everyone, of course, nodded his head to agree with that. But today young people and many older people say, "No, the business of America is far more than business. Business is ruining America, destroying our resources, polluting our air and water."

But what was and is behind the striving for growth and production? Is it greed? Many young people think so, and there may be some of that, but we need to look deeper. The president of Bank of America wrote a fine pamphlet after the burning of one of their branch buildings. He said:

"For centuries—for thousands of years—men struggled just to produce enough to eat, and to produce shelter and clothing. The struggle for just the bare necessities dominated men's lives through most of history. Then, all of a sudden, just within one lifetime, have come all the technological breakthroughs that change all that.

"It was not surprising that we should all get swept up in the excitement of the whole game of producing things. Because there had been such need, here and all over the world, production became the goal, and those who could produce were heroes. Small wonder that there was little thought of what else was happening. If people needed lumber for houses, you cut down trees; and if you needed tractors to get the lumber out, you built factories to build the tractors; and if you needed fuel, you drilled oil wells and built refineries; and you used whatever land was needed, and did whatever you had to do to that land. You not only weren't deliberately doing anything bad, you felt quite virtuous about it—you were a great achiever.

"In fact, through most of history, the concept was that it was a struggle of man against nature; man was trying to conquer nature and the elements, to harness them. So as man acquired mechanical means to do that, he had quite naturally a great sense of triumph. The ones who could do the most of that were the greatest heroes.

"Now we wake up to realize that in the process of 'conquering' nature, we were in fact destroying it—and destroying part of our own lives with it."[1]

That "waking up and realizing" time is upon us. What once was progress is no longer seen as progress. Since life is short, why further shorten it with more pollution? And when the "establishment" says, "Young man, come into our company; keep your nose to the grindstone and work hard, and someday in about thirty years you may be president," the young person today may say, "What for? Who wants to be?"

The new generation is saying (in their highest moments), "Our values are for human dignity—the right to enjoy life." The new mood says, "Let's quit destroying ourselves and our neighbors." I say this is the highest level message that comes through; as we know, there's often a lot of confusion and hatred there, too.

One young person said to me on the campus of our church, "The people of our church don't need big cars that expel their deadly gases. It isn't their right to have those things that do that to their neighbors." And he meant it with all his heart. Those of us of the older generation have no idea how concerned many of the young are about the pollution problem.

Of course, there's the small group of those on one end of the scale who want to burn out the establishment. (One might say, "We'd just like to hand over the system to them and see how they do. They'd learn to appreciate it, and all that's involved in paying the bill.") Then there are young people at the other end of the spectrum who fit into the structure with no problems. But there is in between a great majority who are dissatisfied, really concerned, trying to see a way out.

Now, what are the human solutions? I say "human solutions" because we're hearing them being proposed on all sides. One solution is, "Let the blood flow. Shoot a few, and eventually they'll get the message." But history shows us that repression doesn't just repress the bad guys; it represses everybody. We all lose by violence.

Another human solution has been promoted by reasonable men, not necessarily Christian men, but reasonable. They say, "Let's have a soft voice and willingness to listen to each other—let's communicate." If we're going to communicate, one must talk, one must listen. Two ears; one mouth: that's a good proportion to remember. Young people, they say, need adults. And adults need to open their minds to young people, to listen deeper than the sentence structure may seem to say. Get the feeling behind the words—that's the message.

Recently another very interesting suggestion has come along, an almost unheard little voice amid the clamor. As our planet's troubles deepen and the nations get more desperate, mark my words, this voice will multiply into the roar of the masses. The suggestion is this: our world has gotten too small for each nation to look after its own selfish interests. Too many nations have atomic weapons. Too many nations are dumping their pollutants in other nations' back yards. We need a man—a very strong man—who would have the kind of authority the United Nations has never had. It's too late for discussion. It's too late for red tape. We need a power to whom we will all yield, to save us from destroying ourselves.

As one person says, "What we need is a strong man to make necessary judgments, to find the right line, and have the authority to cause all governments, both large and small, to follow. This person calls for almost superhuman qualities." This statement has already actually been in print.

The Bible says that in the last days a strong world leader claiming all the answers in religion and politics is going to rise up, and the nations will follow. He will be a substitute Christ. He will be the anti-Christ, and eventually, thank God, he will be dealt with by Christ Himself, who will descend upon the world scene and set things right.

Now, those are human solutions. But until Christ comes, what's God's solution to these tremendous rifts between the peoples of the world today?

First of all, certainly the solution must begin with the people of God. The place of unity is in the church, and if it can't be "put together" in the church, it can't be "put together" anywhere.

Think about this: we expect people without Christ to be polarized. But, sad to say, many people in Christ are just as polarized. Tragedy of all tragedies! We see in all of us the tendency to withdraw from each other—to stand over "here" and throw verbal rocks over "there." Even within the body of Christ, we're of Paul, they're of Cephas. Terrible!

Look, our prior commitment is together in the Lord. That commitment to the Body has got to be so exalted that it's 'way up there—far above any other decisions or values. You are not first a Democrat and then a Christian. You're not even an American first. You're not anything else first! You are first Christ's, and Christ's business is to draw us all together. Christian, check your perspective: the higher you go in an airplane, the less walls and fences have anything to do with the scene.

Listen to Romans 12:4,5:

"For as in one body we have many members, and all the members do not have the same function, so we, though many, are one body in Christ, and individually members one of another." (*RSV*)

A young man said to me not long ago, "Older people have to learn to understand us. They don't seem to realize that by next year some of us may well be dead in some war." Well, we do have to try to understand the young—their anxieties and their problems and feelings.

But an older person might well answer him, "You young people don't understand us. We face death more surely than you do. You have no idea of our fears of cancer, or losing our job, or facing the days when usefulness is over."

In today's society, everyone's scrambling to find answers for youth. Well, I think it would be a healthy thing in the body of Christ to see the young people trying to find answers for the older people. How refreshing! Why not—why not?

Look, Paul says, "In the body we have many members." There are young members, old members, poor members, rich members, black members, white members, brown members—there are many members with many functions. "So we, though many, are one body in Christ. . . ." And then—now get this, here's the "clincher"—*"and individually members one of another."* We belong to each other! If it can work in the church, in the family, *in the local church*—the body of Christ can be the showcase to the world that in Christ alone it's possible for humans really to "put it together."

Look at verse 10: "Love one another with brotherly affection; outdo one another in showing honor." Check verse 15: "Rejoice with those who rejoice, weep with those who weep." (*RSV*) That's what happens when you get full of the Holy Spirit, when you're really conquered by Jesus Christ.

We've often said so glibly that if everyone became a Christian, our world's problems would be solved. No, I don't think so at all. As I look at the church, I don't find that true. There are just as many polarizations in the church as there are outside of it. Carnal Christians will no doubt get straightened out in the next world, but they're no help in this one.

Believer, you need to be filled with the Holy Spirit of God, so that you are led by the Spirit, and controlled by the Spirit, and work in the Spirit.

And you need to love the church. Don't let anyone around you "bad-mouth" the church! Some evangelicals think it's cute to say, "I don't believe God is dead. I just think the church is." That's not funny! Build one another up in the faith. Encourage one another in God. Do it! Do it! If God would help us Christians to "put it together," we might become that showcase to the world that could be part of the answer.

Secondly among God's solutions, as individual members of the body of Christ we must go into the world bearing the aroma of peace. "Blessed are the peacemakers," says Jesus. And the last part of Romans 12, verse 19 says,

"Beloved, never avenge yourselves, but leave it to the wrath of God; for it is written, 'Vengeance is mine, I will repay, says the lord' " (*RSV*).

Young people must never become a part of a violent group! Demonstrations are not in the spirit of Romans 12 (or 13). God is the One who will avenge and judge. Trust Him!

And Paul concludes, "If your enemy is hungry, feed him; if he is thirsty, give him drink; for by so doing you will heap burning coals of fire on his head. Do not be overcome by evil, but overcome evil with good" (Rom. 12:20,21, *RSV*).

We need to speak with love—tough love—that says it the best we know how to say it, but says it. I think of Christian school principals and teachers—God bless them!—who are in tough places. Many more laymen need to agonize over their city. How can you be strategic? Where can you infiltrate? May God give us all great courage to be "light" and "salt" in our cities, our suburbs. See how Wisdom in Proverbs 1 stood at the city crossroads; she cried out to the crowds along Main Street. Jesus wept over Jerusalem. Paul preached in the marketplace. How God loves the milling masses of this world!

We're talking about how to cope with today's world. We're looking at the whole scene, and we're asking, "Can it be changed? Is there any hope? Do I just shut my eyes and wait for heaven, or how do I even pray?"

Friend, God's solution may well be a great radical surgery—a mass awakening. We keep longing for this, because of the utter impotence of human solutions. I find myself saying, "Lord, You've just got to come down and really sweep us off our feet; do something dramatic in this day!" Do you say the same thing?

I don't know if He will. I believe in the sovereignty of God in this. But in the past, when revival came to a nation, social issues and world problems were attacked with revived hearts and with clean, new insight. And I do believe that if God would revive the church and really "put us together" in the family, in strong, binding love, we could attack this whole thing of environment problems with new insight—and keen, clean minds.

Out of the evangelical awakening of 1850 in England and America came the ministry of Whitfield, Wesley and others. And then came tremendous power to meet the social needs of the day. As we have many needs, they had many. Racism and slavery, labor problems including child labor, voting rights and all were tremendously helped. And it came out of a spiritual awakening! Revival makes one aware of suffering and of need. In fact, revival and true Christian social action go hand in hand.

I read from our good friend Isaiah, in chapter 58:6-9:

"Is not this the fast that I choose: to loosen the bonds of wickedness, to undo the thongs of the yoke, to let the oppressed go free, and to break every yoke? Is it not to share your bread with the hungry, and bring the homeless poor into your house; when you see the naked, to cover him, and not to hide yourself from your own flesh?" (*RSV*)

Now notice the relationship between loving concern for people and God's special, fresh awakening; they seem to go together—"Then shall your light break forth like the dawn, and your healing shall spring up speedily; your righteousness shall go before you, the glory of the Lord shall be your rear guard. Then you shall call, and the Lord will answer; you shall cry, and He will say, 'Here I am.'"

The people of the world are waiting to be loved!

Lincoln, when he was in New Orleans, saw a mulatto girl on a slave block being pinched and prodded and trotted back and forth like a show horse. He said to his cousin, John Hanks, "If I get in the place where I can hit this thing, I'm going to hit it with all my might!"

He was hated for that. He was killed for that.

A. B. Simpson, founder of the Christian and Missionary Alliance, once was entertaining a house guest. The guest got up early in the morning and unexpectedly happened upon his host. Simpson was sitting at his desk with his arms tightly hugging a large globe of the world. And he was weeping.

Oh, my friend, will you start to love the world? Like that?

Begin planning how to reach the world by straightening out your own life and witness:

1. As you look at your life and relationship to other Christians, how would others evaluate what Christ has to offer? Write it out. Now write out how that witness could be improved.

2. List three ways you could be a "peacemaker" tomorrow—at school, at home, with friends. Ask God to help you do just that.

3. Do you want to love God's world? Then ask Him to give you His love for it.

4. List each person you came in touch with yesterday by name (if you can). Then ask God to make you a better witness of His love to those people next time you meet them.

12

LIVE
BY PRIORITIES

We've talked about three exciting commitments. Maybe your heart has leaped up here and there as you read these words, and you've thought, "I ought to shape up. I ought to take a new look at where I'm going, how my life is turning out. I'm beginning to believe I could be far more than I dreamed. . . ."

My friend, don't put this book down until you've done just that. Have some new thoughts about your life.

You *can* be far more than you dreamed.

But you get just one whack at life. There are no re-runs. You get just one pass through. You can't ever turn back the clock; all you have left is from here on.

Believe—really believe—that God has answers for

you that you maybe didn't even see until now. He promises in Isaiah 42:16, "I will lead them in paths they have not known."

Producers for God get life sorted out. They eliminate in order to concentrate. They set up priorities and put on blinders.

The great King David said, "One thing have I desired of the Lord; that will I seek after."

The apostle Paul wrote, "This one thing I do. . . ."

Are you a little queasy? Do you wonder if you'd become a religious fanatic? George Santayana wrote, "Fanaticism consists of redoubling your efforts when you've forgotten your aim."

Look, you're to aim at God in Christ! You're to zero in on Him and His plan for your individual life. That's not fanaticism; that's just living on target. That's cutting out the clutter. That's "in all things letting Christ have the preeminence." (See Col. 1:18.)

The Living Bible version of Proverbs 16:9 says, "We should make plans—counting on God to direct us."

Then right now make some individual plans, just between you and God, deciding two things:

First, decide what you're going to do.

Second, decide what you're not going to do.

Doesn't that sound simple?

First, what you really want most to do. Your top priorities in three areas: toward God, toward the body of Christ, and toward your work in this world.

Let's be completely practical. If you're going to think through life goals, next week is a definable chunk of your life. Then you could do things next week that would move you on your way to accomplishing those life dreams.

Take a piece of paper and mark it off like this:

Under the left-hand column of priorities, write down your own "God goals"—maybe several—then your "people goals," and then your "work goals." I can't tell you what these will be, but you and God can work them out. They'd certainly include times of daily Bible study and prayer. They would include fellowship with the Body and goals of work accomplishment. Be specific: I want to conquer the book of Ephesians in one month; to learn the art of genuine worship in church; to ask Sue if she feels led to meet weekly with me for study and prayer; to pray over the telephone with Joe every day; to get my room cleaned up and my clothes altered by April 1; to see the person in front of me in English won to Christ by the end of this year; to get the favors done for Joan's party by February 15; to stay caught up on my reading for classes. . . .

Then every day of the week, block in the time when you're going to help these goals to happen.

Think most of all about your "God goals." Consider four things: these blocks of time must be . . .

—prime energy time in the day;

—enough time to accomplish what you want;

—the surest, most realistic time;

—daily! This means the top priority chunks of time may have to shift from day to day, if your days are different, to make sure they're not crowded out.

Next week make another week's schedule.

You may have read *Up the Organization,* that great little book written by the president of Avis Rent-a-Car. ("We're number two; we try harder.") When he first took over as president he said, "We're going to define our objective."

(I have a strong hunch that less than one percent of all Christians have ever sat down with pencil and paper and said, "I'm going to define my life's objective"!)

It took six months for Avis, and when the dust settled they had come up with twenty-three words:

"We want to become the fastest growing company, with the highest profit margin, in the business of renting and leasing vehicles without drivers."

They put it up everywhere—in all the offices, on all the desks. Immediately it became obvious that they'd have to get rid of some branches of the company that didn't fit: "We're going to get rid of everything that doesn't fulfill this. We're going to put blinders on our eyes to everything else."

You know the success story that resulted.

And this brings you to your second decision. You have to decide what you're *not* going to do.

All nature has a sloughing-off process. All that sprouts and lives eventually dies and disintegrates. Otherwise, through the millenniums this globe would have gotten so tightly packed, there'd have been no room for you and me to be born onto it!

Peter Drucker's book *The Effective Executive* says this:

"Above all, the effective executive will slough off an old activity before he starts a new one. This is necessary to keep organizational 'weight control.' Without it the organization soon loses shape, cohesion and manageability. Social organizations need to stay lean and muscular." So must a Christian! Most of us are running pressured lives. We're busy, busy! Then an exciting new project is presented to us: "Will you do so-and-so?" We gasp, "Oh, I couldn't! I'm too busy. I'm too tired!" What we really mean is, "My life is already fat and slow and clogged with too many activities, too much clutter."

Lean, muscular Christians react, "Wow! A new adventure for Jesus. What should go, so that I can do it?"

By the sixth chapter of Acts, the church had grown so fast that the leaders had to say, "What must go, that we can get the top priorities done?" So they sloughed off the feeding program to others, so that they could give themselves to prayer and the ministry of the Word.

They eliminated this, to concentrate on that. They stayed lean!

Now, think carefully, Christian. What should you eliminate? It's disastrous to eliminate the wrong thing! ("I can't go to church Sundays because it's the only day I have to relax.")

Let me suggest the following three things to eliminate:

1. The total failures. This is no problem, because once you've fallen flat on your face, you don't want to do *that* again.

2. Eliminate past successes. Something that was blessed by the Spirit in the past can completely defeat you now. Most churches, most Christians are working so hard at yesterday, they could never cope with today—much less tomorrow.

And yet God's name is "I Am!" He is ever contemporary. He is never ahead, never behind, but He is the only One capable of correctly planning today, because He's the only One who can do it tomorrow. Christian, stay with Him!

3. Eliminate efforts that ought to succeed, but somehow don't. You have this great idea. You struggle and strain. Why doesn't everybody pitch in with you and make it go?

Maybe it's not God's time. Hang loose. If the Spirit isn't pushing something, don't *you* push it.

Here's a "P.S." about what to slough off. Maybe your work activities are all fine, but there are just too many of them. *The Living Bible* version of 1 Corinthians 9:24,25 says:

"In a race, everyone runs but only one person gets first prize. So run your race to win. To win the contest you must deny yourselves many things that would keep you from doing your best. . . ."
Many things that would keep you from Commitment One! Many things that would keep you from Commitment Two!

Maybe you say, "Such-and-such an activity is just too demanding. Another month and we'll have it made, or I can let up a little, but right now, that's just the way it is."

Friend, if you're too busy for God, you're too busy! If you're too busy to attend to the needs of your family, you're too busy! If activities keep you from being a good son or daughter, quit the activity! Find something else.

Activities have to be part of Commitment Three! When you meet God face to face, do you think He is going to ask. "Now, just what was that position that you held with the school club? What was that title again?"

No, no! All that will have been buried forever under the pile of the unimportant.

First Corinthians 3:13 says that the time of testing is coming on the Judgment Day to see what kind of material you built on that foundation which is Christ. And did you ever notice what it is about your life that's going to be judged? Your *ministry!* The quality of the materials of the building for which you were responsible: that is, the quality of the believers in the church as the result of your personal efforts. What kind of discipler were you? Take another look at 1 Corinthians 3 to see that your life will be graded by the spiritual quality of your ministry. That's it, friend. That's what life is all about. God and people.

So you've listed your priorities and goals.

Anybody can make a list. It's like quitting smoking: "It's easy; I've done it a hundred times!"

The point is, *what are you going to quit in life to get these priorities accomplished?*

Your danger and mine is not that we become criminals, but rather that we become respectable, decent, commonplace, mediocre Christians. The twentieth-century temptations that really sap our spiritual power are the television, banana cream pie, the easy chair, and the credit card. The Christian wins or loses in those seemingly innocent little moments of decision.

Lord, make my life a miracle!

FOOTNOTES

Commitment One

1. Thomas Kelly, *A Testament of Devotion* (New York: Harper & Brothers, 1941), p. 115.
2. Frank C. Laubach, *Open Windows, Swinging Doors* (Glendale, California: Regal Books Division, G/L Publications, 1974), pp. 11,12.
3. Thomas Kelly, *A Testament of Devotion,* p. 114.
4. Thomas Kelly, *The Eternal Promise* (New York: Harper & Row, 1966), p. 54.
5. Thomas Kelly, *The Eternal Promise,* p. 115.
6. V. Raymond Edman, *Devotions Are a Delight* (Oradell, New Jersey: American Tract Society).
7. Watchman Nee, *What Shall This Man Do?* (Ft. Washington, Pennsylvania: Christian Literature Crusade, 1965), p. 113.

Commitment Two

1. Bruce Larson, *Setting Men Free* (Grand Rapids: Zondervan Publishing, 1967), p. 119.
2. Bruce Larson, *Setting Men Free,* pp. 119,120.
3. *Christian Education Trends* (Elgin, Illinois: David C. Cook Publishing), September 2, 1968.

Commitment Three

1. Louis B. Lundborg, "The Lessons of Isla Vista," pp. 10,11. From a speech given by Louis B. Lundborg, Chairman of the Board, Bank of America, June 17, 1970.

GRATEFUL RECOGNITION . . .

God has put into my life many choice people who have been like forks in my road.

The *Pastoral Team* of Lake Avenue Congregational Church in Pasadena, California has helped me on to a new way. This book is theirs as much as mine.

I want to acknowledge these brothers and sisters in Christ who want to follow Him into the unfolding future:

Julie Gorman
Robert Hinson
Phyllis Houck
Marvin Jacobs
Bruce Leafblad
Charles Miller
Arlene Nordgren
Harold Peck
Kent Tucker

Raymond C. Ortlund